THE NORTON UTILITIES

Second Edition

KT-153-937

INCLUDES
VERSION 5

Microsoft
PRESS
®

JOHN L. VIESCAS

PUBLISHED BY
Microsoft Press
A Division of Microsoft Corporation
One Microsoft Way
Redmond, Washington 98052-6399

Library of Congress Cataloging-in-Publication Data
Viescas, John, 1947-
    Norton Utilities / John L. Viescas. -- 2nd ed.
        p.   cm. -- (Microsoft quick reference)
    ISBN 1-55615-367-8
    1. Norton Utilities (Computer programs)   I. Title.   II. Series.
QA76.76.U84V54   1991
005.4'3--dc20   90-26328
                                                                    CIP

Printed and bound in the United States of America.

1 2 3 4 5 6 7 8 9   RARA   4 3 2 1 0

Distributed to the book trade in Canada by MacMillan of Canada, a division
of Canada Publishing Corporation.

Distributed to the book trade outside the United States and Canada by Penguin
Books Ltd.

Penguin Books Ltd., Harmondsworth, Middlesex, England
Penguin Books Australia Ltd., Ringwood, Victoria, Australia
Penguin Books N.Z. Ltd., 182–190 Wairau Road, Auckland 10, New Zealand

British Cataloging-in-Publication Data available

Microsoft® and MS-DOS® are registered trademarks and Windows™ is a
trademark of Microsoft Corporation. Norton Utilities®, Norton Disk Doctor®,
WipeFile®, WipeDisk®, and UnErase® are registered trademarks and Speed
Disk™, Disk Monitor™, Calibrat™, Diskreet™, and WipeInfo™ are trademarks
of Peter Norton Computing, Inc.

Acquisitions Editor: Dean Holmes
Project Editor: Editorial Services of New England, Inc.
Technical Editor: Kate Chambers

Contents

Introduction

For each utility in the Norton Utilities versions 3.0 through 5.0, this quick reference guide contains a brief description, complete command line syntax, an explanation of program parameters, and usage notes. Examples are included for the more complex utilities. Entries appear in alphabetic order by command name (for example, DISKTOOL appears before DP (Data Protect)). Appendix A describes common recovery scenarios and suggests utilities you can use, Appendix B provides a sample menu system to enhance your use of MS-DOS with the BE (Batch Enhancer) utility, Appendix C lists the BEEP utility frequency codes for four octaves of the musical scale, and Appendix D contains the color codes you can use when you execute certain utility programs.

Some utilities are not available in all versions. In addition, many utility parameters differ from one version to another. In this guide, the version numbers precede the syntax lines that are valid for those versions. If no syntax line is shown for a particular version number, the utility is not available in that version. Note also that Peter Norton Computing, Inc., and Symantec often add new commands and parameters when they release a maintenance disk for a version. Therefore, your copy of a version might not support all the commands or parameters shown in this guide.

In all versions you can get short, descriptive, on-line help for any command by entering the command name followed by a space and then a single question-mark character, (?). Within interactive menus, you can get context-sensitive help for any command by pressing the F1 key.

Caution for New Users: *If you bought Norton Utilities to restore deleted files or directories, do not copy or install the utilities until you have restored the files or directories. Copying or installing the Norton Utilities could overwrite some of the deleted information.*

Caution for Microsoft Windows Users: *Although you can use many of the Norton Utilities within the Microsoft Windows environment, never run any utility that might move, alter, or destroy any Windows work files or files that are open in an active application. These include CALIBRAT, DISKEDIT, DISKTOOL, DT (Disk Test), FA (File Attributes), FR (Format Recover), NDD (Norton Disk Doctor), NU (Norton Utility), SD (Speed Disk), SF (Safe Format), WIPEDISK, WIPEFILE, and WIPEINFO. In version 5.0, all of these utilities automatically detect the Windows multitasking environment and warn that you should run these utilities only as a single task. If you use the 5.0 utility DISKMON, disable it prior to starting Windows; DISKMON cannot display its dialog box within the Windows environment to determine whether to allow writing over a protected file. See the individual command entries for additional information about running with Windows.*

Caution for 5.0 Users: *If you are upgrading to version 5.0 from version 4.5, be sure to instruct the Install program to place version 5.0 programs in a new directory. In most cases, the version 5.0 Install program will find your version 4.5 directory if you include it in the current path, and it will copy selected utilities from it as noted in this book. Do not select the option to modify your AUTOEXEC.BAT file or activate any of the new version 5.0 terminate-and-stay-resident (TSR) programs until you have tested the new version on your system.*

Syntax Conventions

The conventions listed in the following table describe the Norton Utilities syntax you will encounter in this quick reference guide.

Convention	Meaning
UPPERCASE	Uppercase letters indicate keywords and reserved words that you must enter exactly as shown. Note that you can enter Norton Utility commands in either uppercase or lowercase.

(continued)

(continued)

Convention	Meaning
italic	Italicized words represent variables that you supply.
Brackets [ ]	Brackets enclose optional items, which are separated by a pipe (	) if more than one item is listed. Choose either one or none of the options. Do not enter the brackets or the pipe.
Braces { }	Braces enclose one or more items, which are separated by a pipe (	) if more than one item is listed. You must choose one item from the list. Do not enter the braces or the pipe.
UNDERSCORE	An underscore indicates the minimum number of characters of a keyword you must enter for it to be recognized in its short form.
Ellipses ...	Ellipses indicate that you can repeat an item one or more times. When a comma is shown with ellipses, enter a comma between repetitions of the item.

You must enter all other symbols, such as parentheses and colons, exactly as they appear on the syntax line. Note that in this quick reference guide, *filename* refers to the last qualifier in a pathname, including the file extension. Except where noted, you can use the * and ? wildcard characters. The *path* parameter refers to the list of directory and sub-directory names that qualify the location of *filename*.

Commands

ASK

Description:

Displays a prompt message and then awaits single-key input. You can supply a list of keys that defines the key response that ASK will accept. If you provide *keylist*, the command returns an MS-DOS ERRORLEVEL, which you can test with an IF batch command to control the flow of commands in a batch command file.

Syntax:

4.0   ASK *prompt*[,*keylist*]

4.5, 5.0   *See* BE ASK

Parameters:

prompt A character string ASK displays before waiting for input. You do not need to enclose the prompt in quotation marks unless it contains either a comma or a single or double quotation mark.

keylist A list of the character keys, number keys, or symbol keys that ASK will accept as a response. The list must be a single string of characters with no intervening spaces. When you supply *keylist*, ASK returns ERRORLEVEL based on the position in the list of the key the user presses; that is, pressing the first key in the list sets ERRORLEVEL equal to 1, pressing the second key sets ERRORLEVEL equal to 2, and so on. If you do not specify *keylist*, pressing any key completes execution of the utility with ERRORLEVEL set to 0.

5

Notes:

- The MS-DOS batch command IF ERRORLEVEL *n* evaluates to true whenever *n* is less than or equal to the current ERRORLEVEL. To obtain the results you want from a set of IF ERRORLEVEL commands, test for the highest possible ERRORLEVEL first. See the example below.

- The ASK command is available only in version 4.0. ASK is incorporated into the BE (Batch Enhancer) utility in versions 4.5 and later.

Example:

To prompt the user with a choice either to continue in a batch file or to quit, enter

```
ASK Enter C to continue or Q to quit: ,CQ
IF ERRORLEVEL 2 GOTO QUIT
:CONTINUE

    .
    .
    .

  additional commands
:QUIT
REM Last line in the batch file
```

See also: BE ASK, Appendix B.

BE (Batch Enhancer)

Description:

Provides subcommands you can use in a batch file to enhance interaction with a user. Subcommands are available to prompt for input, to sound tones on the internal speaker, to display messages at specific locations, to draw boxes and windows on the screen, and to control the colors of the screen display. See the BE subcommand descriptions that follow.

Syntax:

4.5, 5.0   BE *subcommand* ?

BE *subcommand parameters*

BE [*drive*:][*path*]*filename*

Parameters:

subcommand The name of the Batch Enhancer subcommand. Note that you can get brief help text for each subcommand by entering the subcommand name followed by a
space and then a question-mark character (?).

drive: The single-letter designator for the drive that contains
the Batch Enhancer command file. Follow the letter with a
colon. The current drive is the default.

path The fully qualified name of the directory that contains
the Batch Enhancer command file. The current directory for
the designated drive is the default.

filename The name of the file that contains a series of Batch
Enhancer subcommands to be executed. BE ignores empty
lines in the file. You can include a comment by beginning a
line with REM. You can prefix each subcommand in the file
with the BE command; that is, BE BEEP is the same as
BEEP.

See also: BE ASK, BE BEEP, BE BOX, BE CLS, BE
DELAY, BE GOTO, BE PRINTCHAR, BE ROWCOL,
BE SA, BE WINDOW, Appendix B.

BE ASK

Description:

Displays a prompt message and then awaits single-key input.
You can supply a list of keys that defines the key response
BE ASK will accept, as well as a default key value, a
timeout interval, and color attributes for the prompt message.

If you provide *keylist*, BE ASK returns ERRORLEVEL, which you can test with an IF batch command to control the flow of commands in a batch command file. If you are nesting BE ASK commands within a menu system, you can adjust the ERRORLEVEL that is returned to determine which menu set the returned code.

Syntax:

4.5, 5.0   BE ASK "*prompt*"[[,]*keylist*] [DEFAULT=*key*]
              [TIMEOUT=*n*] [ADJUST=*n*] [[BLINKING]
              [BRIGHT | BOLD] [*text-color*] [[ON] *back-color*]]

Parameters:

prompt A character string BE ASK displays before waiting for input. You must enclose the prompt in quotation marks if it includes one or more blank spaces. If the prompt contains a single quotation mark character, enclose the prompt in double quotation marks. If the prompt contains a double quotation mark character, enclose the prompt in single quotation marks.

keylist A list of the character keys, number keys, or symbol keys that will be accepted as a response. The list must be a single string of characters with no intervening spaces. In early copies of version 5.0, *keylist* is required if you want to include any other keywords. When you supply *keylist*, BE ASK sets ERRORLEVEL based on the position in the list of the key you choose; that is, pressing the first key in the list sets ERRORLEVEL equal to 1, pressing the second key sets ERRORLEVEL equal to 2, and so on. If you press a key not in *keylist*, BE ASK beeps and waits for a proper response. If you do not specify *keylist*, pressing any key completes execution of BE ASK with ERRORLEVEL set to 0.

DEFAULT=*key* The key in *keylist* that BE ASK uses if the optional timeout elapses or if you press Enter.

TIMEOUT=*n* A time interval, in seconds, that BE ASK waits before completing execution. If you specify a default key and if the time interval expires, BE ASK returns the ERRORLEVEL value corresponding to that key. If you do

not specify a default key, BE ASK sets the ERRORLEVEL
value of the last key in *keylist*; if you do not specify *keylist*,
BE ASK sets a value of 0.

ADJUST=*n* A numeric value BE ASK adds to the returned
ERRORLEVEL code to adjust for stacked menus.

BLINKING Causes the prompt message to blink on and off
repeatedly. On some monitors, this keyword works only if
you specify *back-color*.

BRIGHT | **BOLD** Displays the prompt message in high
intensity.

text-color Specifies the color of the text of the prompt message and the response character. The default is the current
foreground color setting for the screen area that is covered
by the text. See BE SA.

back-color Specifies the color of the background block for
the prompt message and for the response character. If you do
not provide *text-color*, you must include the ON keyword.
The default is the current background setting for the screen
area that is covered by the text. See BE SA.

Notes:

■ The MS-DOS batch command IF ERRORLEVEL *n* evaluates to true whenever *n* is less than or equal to the current ERRORLEVEL. To obtain the results you want from
a set of IF ERRORLEVEL commands, test for the highest
possible ERRORLEVEL first. See the example below.

■ The BE ASK command in versions 4.5 and later replaces
the ASK command available in version 4.0.

Example:

To display a bright-red-on-green prompt that provides a
choice between continuing in a batch file and quitting, with a
default value of Q if the user does not respond within 20
seconds, enter

```
BE ASK "Enter C to continue or Q to quit: ",CQ
 D=Q T=20 BRI RED ON GREEN
IF ERRORLEVEL 2 GOTO QUIT
:CONTINUE

   .
   .
   .

  additional commands
:QUIT
REM Last line in the batch file
```

See also: BE, BE SA, Appendix B, Appendix D.

BE BEEP

Description:

Sounds a tone or series of tones on the system's internal
speaker. A tone is defined by a frequency and a duration.

Syntax:

4.5, 5.0   BE BEEP [*drive:*][*path*]*filename* [/E]

           BE BEEP [/F*n*] [/D*n*] [/R*n*] [/W*n*]

Parameters:

drive: The single-letter designator for the drive that contains
the file you want to use. Follow the letter with a colon. The
current drive is the default.

path The fully qualified name of the directory in which the
file is defined. The current directory for the designated drive
is the default.

filename The name of the file that contains tone values
BE BEEP can sound. Each line in the file can contain frequency (/F), duration (/D), repetition (/R), and wait (/W)
specification parameters. Each line in the file can contain a
comment; specify the beginning of a comment with a semi-

colon. Within a comment, BE BEEP displays any words enclosed in double quotation marks as it plays each note. See
the example below.

/D*n* Specifies the duration of the sound in eighteenths of a
second; for example, /D18 sounds the frequency for one second. The number must be a positive integer. If you specify
neither the /D parameter nor the /F parameter (see below),
BE BEEP sounds the computer's default tone. If you specify
/F without specifying /D, the frequency sounds for approximately one-half second (/D9).

/E If you specify *filename*, causes BE BEEP to display any
comments that are enclosed in double quotation marks.

/F*n* Specifies the frequency of the sound in cycles per second. The number must be a positive integer. Middle C is approximately 262. See Appendix C for an extensive list of
frequencies. If you do not specify this parameter, BE BEEP
sounds the computer's default frequency.

/R*n* Specifies the number of times BE BEEP repeats the
sound. The number must be a positive integer.

/W*n* Specifies the wait interval at the end of each tone in
eighteenths of a second. The number must be a positive integer. Note that if you specify the /R parameter, no sound
occurs during the wait interval at the end of each repetition
of the tone.

Example:

To play the song "Three Blind Mice" from a stored file and
to display the words as the notes are played, enter

```
BE BEEP mice.dat /E
```

File MICE.DAT contains

```
;    Three Blind Mice
;    Freq. Dur. Wait Rep.    Note    Words:
BEEP F659  D10              ; E      "Three"
BEEP F587  D10              ; D      "Blind"
BEEP F523  D10  W10         ; C      "Mice.  "
BEEP F659  D10              ; E      "Three"
BEEP F587  D10              ; D      "Blind"
```

```
BEEP  F523  D10   W10           ;  C         "Mice.  "
BEEP  F784  D10                 ;  G         "See"
BEEP  F698  D5          /R2 ;  F, F      "How They"
BEEP  F659  D10   W10           ;  E         "Run!"
BEEP  F784  D10                 ;  G         "See"
BEEP  F698  D5          /R2 ;  F, F      "How They"
BEEP  F659  D10   W10           ;  E         "Run!"
```

See also: Appendix C.

BE BOX

Description:

Displays a box outline on the screen and does not overlay
any data inside the box.

Syntax:

4.5, 5.0   BE BOX *top-row*[,] *left-col*[,] *bottom-row*[,] *right-col*
[DOUBLE | SINGLE] [[BLINKING] [BRIGHT |
BOLD] [*line-color*] [[ON] *back-color*]]

Parameters:

top-row The row on the screen where you want to display
the top line of the box. The number of the first row is 0.

left-col The column on the screen where you want to
display the left line of the box. The number of the first
column is 0.

bottom-row The row on the screen where you want to
display the bottom line of the box. The last row on most
standard (25-line) screens is 24, but some adapters can display more rows. For example, if you have a VGA adapter
and have set the screen to 50 rows with NCC /50, the last
row is 49. The *bottom-row* value must be greater than the
top-row value.

right-col The column on the screen where you want to display the right line of the box. The last column number is 79.
The *right-col* value must be greater than the *left-col* value.

DOUBLE | SINGLE Specifies either a double-line box or a single-line box. The default value is DOUBLE.

BLINKING Causes the box to blink on and off repeatedly. On some monitors, this keyword works only if you specify *back-color*.

BRIGHT | BOLD Displays the box lines in high intensity.

line-color Specifies the color of the box lines. The default is the current foreground color setting for the screen. After BE BOX executes, any characters you display within the box border using other BE commands, such as BE ASK or BE ROWCOL, appear in *line-color*. If you use an MS-DOS command such as ECHO or TYPE to display characters, the characters appear on the screen in the original foreground and background colors.

back-color Specifies the color of the background frame for the box lines. If you do not provide *line-color*, you must include the ON keyword. The default is the current background setting for the screen. After BE BOX executes, any characters you display within the box border using other BE commands, such as BE ASK or BE ROWCOL, appear on a background of *back-color*. If you use an MS-DOS command such as ECHO or TYPE to display characters, those characters appear in the original foreground and background colors.

Example:

To display a box that is large enough to contain a 9-column-by-5-row area of data in the upper left corner of the screen, and to make the box appear as blinking, green double lines on a black border, and to display **ERROR** inside the box, enter

```
BE BOX 0, 0, 6, 10 DOUBLE BLINKING GREEN ON BLACK
BE ROWCOL 3, 1 "**ERROR**"
```

See also: BE SA, BE WINDOW, NCC, Appendix B, Appendix D.

BE CLS (Clear Screen)

Description:

Sets the background color to black, erases the screen, and then resets the original background color.

Syntax:

4.5, 5.0   BE CLS

Note:

■ The MS-DOS CLS command erases only the characters displayed on the screen, leaving the background color unaffected. BE CLS sets the background color to black before erasing the screen; this might be useful for subsequent BE BOX or BE ROWCOL displays. Note that if you subsequently use an MS-DOS command such as ECHO or TYPE to display data, the data appears in the original foreground and background colors.

See also: BE BOX, BE ROWCOL, BE WINDOW.

BE DELAY

Description:

Waits for a specified amount of time between commands in a batch file to let the user see a message or a screen display. The batch file resumes execution after the pause.

Syntax:

4.5, 5.0   BE DELAY *n*

Parameters:

n An amount of time to wait, in eighteenths of a second.

Example:

To display a message in the center of the screen and then pause for five seconds to let the user see the message before the batch command file resumes execution, enter

```
BE ROWCOL 12,30 "You have 5 seconds to read this."
BE DELAY 90
```

BE GOTO

Description:

Branches to the specified label within a Batch Enhancer command file or to the Batch Enhancer command file specified by the path and filename parameters.

Syntax:

5.0   In an MS-DOS batch file:

BE [*drive:*][*path*]*filename*[[GOTO]*label*]

Within a Batch Enhancer command file:

GOTO *label*

Parameters:

drive: The single-letter designator for the drive that contains the Batch Enhancer command file. Follow the letter with a colon. The current drive is the default.

path The fully qualified name of the directory that contains the Batch Enhancer command file. The current directory for the designated drive is the default.

filename The name of the file that contains Batch Enhancer subcommands.

label The identifier for the position in the Batch Enhancer command file where you want execution to resume. You

must precede the *label* in a Batch Enhancer command file
with a colon. You may include comments after the identifier
in the batch file (see the example below).

Caution: *If the label you specify does not exist in the Batch
Enhancer command file, the BE utility may stop your computer.*

Example:

To display a selected window based on the response to a
BE ASK command, enter

```
BE ASK "Select Window 1 or 2: ",12
IF ERRORLEVEL 2 GOTO SHOW2
:SHOW1
BE C:\MENUS\BOXES.DAT GOTO BOX1
GOTO DONE
:SHOW2
BE C:\MENUS\BOXES.DAT GOTO BOX2
:DONE
```

BOXES.DAT contains

```
:BOX1    Display box 1
BOX 5,10,20,60 BRI RED ON GREEN

.
.
.

GOTO EXIT
:BOX2    Display box 2
BOX 15,5,22,50 MAG ON BLUE

.
.
.

:EXIT
```

See also: BE.

BE PRINTCHAR

Description:

Displays a repeated single character, beginning at the current cursor location. You can reposition the cursor with the BE ROWCOL command.

Syntax:

4.5, 5.0   BE PRINTCHAR *char*[,] *count* [[BLINKING]
              [BRIGHT | BOLD] [*char-color*] [[ON] *back-color*]]

Parameters:

char The single character you want to display. You can enclose the character in single or double quotation marks. If you provide more than one character, BE PRINTCHAR repeats only the first one. Note that you cannot use the question mark character (?) for *char* and you must enclose the special characters | ; < > and / in double quotation marks.

count The number of times you want *char* to appear on the screen. Repeated characters beyond the end of a line wrap to the next line.

BLINKING Causes the characters to blink on and off repeatedly. On some monitors, this keyword works only if you specify *back-color*.

BRIGHT | BOLD Displays the characters in high intensity.

char-color Specifies the color of the characters. The default is the current foreground color setting for the screen area that is covered by the characters. See BE SA.

back-color Specifies the color of the background for the characters. If you do not provide *char-color*, you must include the ON keyword. The default is the current background setting for the screen area that the characters cover. See BE SA.

See also: BE ROWCOL, BE SA, Appendix D.

BE ROWCOL

Description:

Repositions the cursor on the screen and can also
display text.

Syntax:

4.5, 5.0   BE ROWCOL *row*[,] *col* [[,] *text* [[BLINKING]
                [BRIGHT | BOLD] [*text-color*] [[ON] *back-color*]]]

Parameters:

row The row on the screen where you want to position the
cursor. The first row is 0. The last row on most standard (25-
line) screens is 24, but some adapters can display more rows.

col The column in the specified row where you want to
position the cursor. The first column is 0, and the last
column is 79.

text An optional message you want to display at the specified cursor location. You must enclose a message in either
single or double quotation marks if it includes one or more
blank spaces.

BLINKING Causes *text* to blink on and off repeatedly.
On some monitors, this keyword works only if you specify
back-color.

BRIGHT | BOLD Displays text in high intensity.

text-color Specifies the color of text. The default is the current foreground color setting for the screen area that is covered by *text*. See BE SA.

back-color Specifies the color of the background for the
message. If you do not provide *text-color*, you must include
the ON keyword. The default is the current background setting for the screen area that the text covers. See BE SA.

See also: BE SA, NCC, Appendix B, Appendix D.

BE SA (Screen Attributes)

Description:
Sets screen attributes.

Syntax:
4.5   BE SA {NORMAL | REVERSE | UNDERLINE} [/N]

BE SA {[[BLINKING] [BRIGHT | BOLD]] [*fore-color*]
[[ON] *back-color*]} [/N] [/C]

5.0   BE SA {NORMAL | REVERSE | UNDERLINE} [/N]

BE SA {[[BLINKING] [BRIGHT | BOLD]] [*fore-color*]
[[ON] *back-color*]} [/N] [/CLS]

Parameters:
BLINKING Causes text to blink on and off repeatedly.
On some monitors, this keyword works only if you specify
back-color.

BRIGHT | BOLD Sets the foreground color to high
intensity.

NORMAL Resets the screen to the standard colors for your
display adapter and erases the screen.

REVERSE Sets the screen display to reverse video and
erases the screen.

UNDERLINE Sets the screen display to underline mode
and erases the screen. On some display adapters, this
keyword resets the default to color characters on a black
background.

fore-color Specifies the foreground color for screen displays
such as messages, box lines, and window-frame lines. The
default color is white.

back-color Specifies the background color for screen displays. If you do not provide *fore-color*, you must include the
ON keyword. The default color is black.

/C Clears the screen after you set new screen attributes.

/CLS Clears the screen after you set new screen attributes.

/N Does not reset the border color when the display is in either CGA mode or VGA mode. This switch does not affect EGA display mode.

Notes:

■ To use this utility, you must install the ANSI.SYS driver.

■ In versions 4.5 and later, BE SA replaces the version 4.0 SA (Screen Attributes) utility.

See also: NCC, Appendix B, Appendix D.

BE WINDOW

Description:

Displays a window that is framed with a double line. The window overlays any data inside it.

Syntax:

4.5, 5.0   BE WINDOW *top-row*[,] *left-col*[,] *bottom-row*[,] *right-col*
[[BLINKING] [BRIGHT | BOLD] [*frame-color*]
[[ON] *fill-color*]] [SHADOW] [ZOOM]

Parameters:

top-row The row on the screen where you want to display the top of the window. The number of the first row is 0.

left-col The column on the screen where you want to display the left side of the window. The number of the first column is 0.

bottom-row The row on the screen where you want to display the bottom of the window. The last row on most standard (25-line) screens is 24, but some adapters can display more rows. For example, if you have a VGA adapter

and have set the screen to 50 rows with NCC /50, the last
row is 49. The *bottom-row* value must be greater than the
top-row value.

right-col The column on the screen where you want to
display the right side of the window. The last column number is 79. The *right-col* value must be greater than the *left-
col* value.

BLINKING Causes the frame to blink on and off
repeatedly.

BRIGHT | **BOLD** Displays the window-frame lines in high
intensity.

frame-color Specifies the color of the window-frame lines.
The default is the current foreground color setting for the
screen. After BE WINDOW executes, any characters you
display in the window using other BE commands, such as
BE ASK or BE ROWCOL, appear in *frame-color*. If you use
an MS-DOS command such as ECHO or TYPE to display
characters, the characters appear in the original screen foreground and background colors. See BE SA.

fill-color Specifies the background color of the window. If
you do not provide *frame-color*, you must include the ON
keyword. The default color is black. After BE WINDOW executes, any characters you display in the window using other
BE commands, such as BE ASK or BE ROWCOL, appear
on a background of *fill-color*. If you use an MS-DOS command such as ECHO or TYPE to display characters, the
characters appear in the original screen foreground and
background colors.

SHADOW Creates a transparent, gray shadow on the right
and bottom sides of the window. Any characters that the
shadow covers are still visible. The shadow may not be visible on LCD screens.

ZOOM Causes the window to appear to zoom out from the
center of the window. The zoom effect may not be apparent
on very fast machines.

Example:

To display a window that is large enough to contain a 30-column-by-9-row area of data in the center of a standard (25-line-by-80-character) screen and that appears as a black frame on a green background, enter

```
BE WINDOW 7 24 17 55 BLACK ON GREEN
```

See also: BE BOX, BE SA, NCC, Appendix B, Appendix D.

BEEP

Description:

Sounds a tone or a series of tones on the system's internal speaker. A tone consists of a frequency and a duration.

Syntax:

3.0 BEEP

3.1 BEEP [/F*n*] [/D*n*] [/R*n*]

4.0 BEEP [/F*n*] [/D*n*] [/R*n*] [/W*n*]

BEEP [*drive*:][*path*] *filename*

4.5, 5.0 *See* BE BEEP

Parameters:

drive: The single-letter designator for the drive that contains the file you want to use. Follow the letter with a colon. The current drive is the default.

path The fully qualified name of the directory that contains the file you want to use. The current directory for the designated drive is the default.

filename The name of the file that contains tone values BEEP can sound. Each line in the file can contain frequency (/F), duration (/D), repetition (/R), and wait (/W) specification parameters. Each line in the file can contain a comment; specify the beginning of a comment with a semicolon. See the example under BE BEEP.

/D*n* Specifies the duration of the sound in eighteenths of a second; for example, /D18 sounds the frequency for one second. The number must be an integer. If you specify neither the /D parameter nor the /F parameter (see the following page), BEEP sounds the computer's default tone. If you specify /F without specifying /D, the frequency sounds for approximately one-half second (/D9).

/F*n* Specifies the frequency of the sound in cycles per second. The number must be an integer. Middle C is approximately 262. See Appendix C for an extensive list of frequencies. If you do not specify this parameter, BEEP sounds the computer's default frequency.

/R*n* Specifies the number of times BEEP repeats the tone. The number must be a positive integer.

/W*n* Specifies the wait interval at the end of each tone in eighteenths of a second. The number must be a positive integer. Note that if you specify the /R parameter, no sound occurs during the wait interval at the end of each repetition of the tone.

Note:

■ The BEEP command is incorporated into the BE (Batch Enhancer) utility in versions 4.5 and later.

See also: BE BEEP.

CALIBRAT

Description:
Tests system, disk controller, and hard drive integrity; validates data recorded on hard disks; and can alter the interleave on a hard drive to optimize data access.

Syntax:

5.0 CALIBRAT [*drive*:][/<u>BA</u>TCH] [/<u>BL</u>ANK]
[/<u>NOCO</u>PY][/<u>NO</u>FORMAT] [/<u>NOSEEK</u>]
[/<u>P</u>ATTERN:*n*][/R:*filename* | /RA:*filename*][/X:*drvltrs*]

Parameters:

drive: The single-letter designator for the hard drive you
want to process. Follow the letter with a colon. The current
drive is the default. If the current drive is not a hard drive or
you specify a drive that is not a hard drive, CALIBRAT
prompts you for a drive to process from the available hard
drives on the system.

/<u>BA</u>TCH Skips all prompts. Use this switch when you want
CALIBRAT to execute to completion without pausing (for
example, in a batch file). If the drive you specify is not a
hard drive or is not valid, CALIBRAT prompts you for a
drive to process even if you include this switch.

/<u>BL</u>ANK Causes CALIBRAT to start pattern testing with
the screen blank. Pattern testing can take a long time, especially if you request /PATTERN:40 or /PATTERN:80; this
option helps prevent screen burn-in. You can use the
spacebar during pattern testing to turn the screen display on
and off even if you do not use /<u>BL</u>ANK.

/<u>NOCO</u>PY Requests that CALIBRAT not make a backup
copy of each track as it is processed during pattern testing
and low-level formatting. This option significantly reduces
execution time while only slightly increasing the risk of loss
of data in the event of a catastrophic system failure (such as
a sudden power loss).

/<u>NO</u>FORMAT Skips interleave testing. CALIBRAT will
not perform any low-level formatting to improve disk interleave during the final pattern testing phase.

/<u>NOSEEK</u> Skips seek testing.

/<u>P</u>ATTERN:*n* Specifies the level of pattern testing required. Valid values for *n* are 0, 5, 40, and 80, each indicating the number of patterns CALIBRAT uses to test each

track. A value of 0 (the default) requests only simple read/write testing. Use 0 if you want only to adjust disk interleave quickly. If you specify 80, the full pattern test may run many hours on a large disk.

/R:*filename* Produces a report about the results of running CALIBRAT and stores it in the named file if you include /BATCH or if you select Save As when prompted. The *filename* can include a drive and a path. If the file does not already exist, CALIBRAT creates it. If the file already exists, CALIBRAT overwrites it without first prompting you for confirmation.

/RA:*filename* Produces a report about the results of running CALIBRAT and appends it to the named file if you include /BATCH or if you select Save As when prompted. The *filename* can include a drive and a path. If the file does not already exist, CALIBRAT creates it.

/X:*drvltrs* Excludes specified drives from testing. Some manufacturers' versions of MS-DOS allocate drive letters to disk drives that do not exist; use this switch to inform CALIBRAT that these drive letters are invalid.

Notes:

■ Back up your hard drive before running CALIBRAT for the first time. After you have determined that CALIBRAT is compatible with your hardware, you can safely run CALIBRAT without first backing up the disk.

■ CALIBRAT does not work with floppy drives, network drives, or any drive that uses a sector size other than 512 KB. CALIBRAT can run many tests but may not be able to perform low-level formatting on certain other drives (such as those with SCSI or IDE controllers). CALIBRAT skips format analysis on drives it determines it cannot reformat.

See also: NCACHE-F, NCACHE-S, SPEEDISK.

DI (Disk Information)

Description:

Displays technical information about a disk drive. The information includes device type, drive number, bytes per sector, sectors per cluster, number of file allocation tables (FATs), and so on.

Syntax:

4.0, 4.5   DI [*drive*:]

5.0   *See* SYSINFO

Parameters:

drive: The single-letter designator for the drive you want to process. Follow the letter with a colon. The current drive is the default. If you are using a floppy drive, you must have a formatted disk in the drive to receive complete information.

Notes:

■ DI returns an encoded media descriptor value to describe the disk type. The following table lists and defines the values that are valid:

Hex value	Meaning
F0	1.4-MB 3½-inch floppy disk
F8	Hard disk (all types)
F9	1.2-MB 5¼-inch floppy disk or 720-KB 3½-inch floppy disk
FD	360-KB 5¼-inch floppy disk
FE	160-KB 5¼-inch floppy disk
FF	320-KB 5¼-inch floppy disk

■ For the drive number, the utility returns 0 for drive A, 1 for drive B, and so on.

■ DI is incorporated into the SYSINFO command in version 5.0.

DISKEDIT

Description:
Runs a full-screen utility that displays information about a disk and lets you scan and edit information on a disk.

Syntax:
5.0   DISKEDIT [*drive:*][*path:*][*filename*] [/M] [/X:*drvltrs*]

Parameters:

drive: The single-letter designator for the drive you want to process. Follow the letter with a colon. The current drive is the default.

path The fully qualified name of the directory to process. The current directory is the default.

filename The name of the file you want to display. If the *filename* you supply does not exist, DISKEDIT displays the contents of *path*. The default *filename* is *.*.

/M Sets maintenance mode to allow DISKEDIT to bypass the MS-DOS logical structure. Use this switch if you are working with a badly damaged disk.

/X:*drvltrs* Excludes specified drives from testing. Some manufacturers' versions of MS-DOS allocate drive letters to disk drives that do not exist; use this switch to inform DISKEDIT that these drive letters are invalid.

Notes:

■ When you install Norton Utilities Version 5.0, one option gives DISKEDIT a short name of DE. If you used the shortened name use DE instead of DISKEDIT in the syntax line above.

■ You can use DISKEDIT to search files, directories, or sectors for specific information, to display information about items you have selected, and to display data that is on your disk in hexadecimal, text, or directory format. When your data is displayed in hexadecimal format, you can modify it and request DISKEDIT to write it back to disk. You can also change your data when it is in directory format display mode, you can edit and change the file allocation table (FAT) and the partition table, and you can scan the disk by absolute cluster address.

Caution: *If you make changes to data in directories, in the FAT, in the partition table, or in the boot record, you can lose data or render your disk unusable.*

■ You can use the following shortcut key combinations in DISKEDIT:

Key	Function
Alt-A	Select the partition table
Alt-B	Select the boot record
Alt-C	Select a cluster
Alt-D	Select a drive
Alt-F	Select a file
Alt-P	Select a physical sector
Alt-R	Select a directory
Alt-S	Select a sector
Ctrl-B	Mark a block to copy or fill
Ctrl-C	Copy to clipboard
Ctrl-D	Link FAT entry or file to related directory entry
Ctrl-F	Link FAT entry or directory entry to related file
Ctrl-G	Find again
Ctrl-Q	Quit
Ctrl-S	Find
Ctrl-T	Link directory entry or file to FAT entry
Ctrl-U	Undo changes
Ctrl-V	Paste from clipboard
Ctrl-W	Write changes
F2	View as hex
F3	View as text
F4	View as directory

(continued)

(continued)

Key	Function
F5	View as FAT
F6	View as partition table
F7	View as boot record
Alt-F1	Select first FAT
Alt-F2	Select second FAT
Shift-F5	Split/unsplit window
Shift-F6	Grow window
Shift-F7	Shrink window
Shift-F8	Switch windows

See also: DISKTOOL, NORTON, NU, UNERASE.

DISKMON

Description:

Monitors disk access, optionally displays a disk access symbol in the upper right corner of the screen, and protects specified files from being overwritten or deleted. You can also use DISKMON to park hard drive heads prior to turning off your computer.

Syntax:

5.0   DISKMON [/LIGHT{+|-}] [/PARK] [/PROTECT{+|-}]
         [/STATUS] [/UNINSTALL]

Parameters:

/LIGHT+ Turns on display of the disk access symbol.

/LIGHT− Turns off display of the disk access symbol.

/PARK Parks your hard drive heads. DISKMON honors this parameter first. If you press any key after DISKMON parks the heads, DISKMON honors any other parameters before returning you to the command line prompt.

/PROTECT+ Activates protection of files.

/**PROTECT**– Deactivates protection of files.

/**STATUS** Displays current protect and light status.

/**UNINSTALL** Removes DISKMON from memory.

Notes:

■ DISKMON is a terminate-and-stay-resident (TSR) program. If you plan to run DISKMON all the time, include the command DISKMON /PROTECT+ /LIGHT+ in your AUTOEXEC.BAT file.

■ When you have activated file protection, DISKMON by default protects all BIN, COM, EXE, OVL, and SYS files from being deleted or overwritten. This provides excellent protection against inadvertently deleting important files. It also helps protect against virus infection. You can open a dialog box that lets you define different file protection by entering the DISKMON command with no parameters.

■ When you have protected files, DISKMON displays a dialog box requesting you to authorize any deletion of or writing to protected files as long as the screen is in character mode. When the screen is in graphics mode (for example, when running under Microsoft Windows 3.0), DISKMON cannot display the dialog box. Instead, DISKMON sounds a low tone and does not allow access to the file. For this reason, you may need to deactivate DISKMON file protection before attempting to run certain Windows 3.0 programs.

■ When you use /LIGHT to activate disk access display, DISKMON flashes the drive letter with a right arrow for read operations and the drive letter with a left arrow for write operations in the upper left corner of your screen when the screen is in character mode. If your monitor is in graphics mode, DISKMON cannot display the symbol.

DISKREET

Description:

Secures files by encrypting them. You can use DISKREET
to encrypt individual files, or you can load DISKREET as a
device driver and set up hidden areas on one or more disks
that can be opened as logical drives and used to encrypt and
store one or more files. Norton calls these hidden areas
NDisks.

Syntax:

5.0   In CONFIG.SYS:

DEVICE=[*drive:*][*path*]DISKREET.SYS [/A20ON]
[/NOHMA] [/SKIPUMB]

From the command line:

DISKREET [/CLOSE | [{/ENCRYPT:[*drive:*][*path*]*filename* |
/DECRYPT:[*drive:*][*path*]*filename*} [/PASSWORD:*pswd*]] |
/HIDE:[*drive*] | /ON | /OFF | /SHOW:[*drive*]]

Parameters:

drive: The single-letter designator for the drive you
want to process. Follow the letter with a colon except in
the /HIDE and /SHOW parameters. The current drive is
the default.

path The fully qualified name of the directory that contains
the *filename* you want to process. The current directory is
the default.

filename The name of the file you want to encrypt or
decrypt.

/A20ON Eliminates overhead of enabling/disabling the A20
line. Use this switch if you experience network problems or
a loss of data during serial communications while using
High Memory Area (HMA).

/CLOSE Closes any open logical drives that are allocated to an NDisk.

/DECRYPT:[*drive:*][*path*] *filename* Requests that the specified file be decrypted. If you do not specify a password (/PASSWORD:), DISKREET prompts you for the password and does not display what you enter.

/ENCRYPT:[*drive:*][*path*] *filename* Requests that the specified file be encrypted. If you do not specify a password (/PASSWORD:), DISKREET prompts you for the password and does not display what you enter. DISKREET automatically changes the file extension to SEC when it encrypts the file. If this creates a duplicate filename, DISKREET prompts you for a name. Enter a unique name with the extension SEC in response to the prompt.

/HIDE:[*drive*] Scans the specified drive for NDisk files and sets the Hidden attribute to hide them. If you do not specify a drive letter, DISKREET scans the current drive.

/NOHMA Prevents DISKREET from using the High Memory Area (HMA). Include this switch to prevent high memory conflicts if you are using Microsoft Windows. You must have an XMS driver such as HIMEM.SYS installed before DISKREET can use HMA. If you allow DISKREET to use High Memory, it uses less than 12 KB of low (below 640 KB) memory.

/OFF Closes all logical drives assigned to an NDisk and disables the installed DISKREET device driver.

/ON Enables the DISKREET device driver if it is installed but has been disabled with /OFF.

/PASSWORD:*pswd* Specifies the password used to encrypt or decrypt files.

/SHOW:[*drive*] Scans the specified drive for NDisk files and resets the hidden attribute. DISKREET stores NDisk files with the extension @#!. If you do not specify a drive letter, DISKREET scans the current drive.

/SKIPUMB Prevents DISKREET from using any memory
that exists in an Upper Memory Block above 640 KB but
below the High Memory Area (HMA). If you use a memory
manager such as 386-MAX or QEMM to load programs into
upper memory, you may want to include this switch to avoid
memory usage conflicts. If you allow DISKREET to use
upper memory, it uses less than 1 KB of low memory (below
640 KB).

Notes:

■ You must supply a file password to decrypt an individual
   file, and individual files must be decrypted before you
   can use them.

■ You must first install DISKREET as a device driver in
   CONFIG.SYS (see CONFIG.SYS command line above)
   before you can use an encrypted disk area (NDisk) as a
   logical drive. Also, DISKREET does not honor the command line parameters /CLOSE, /HIDE, /ON, /OFF, or
   /SHOW unless you have installed the device driver. After
   the device driver is active, use DISKREET with no oper-
   ands to activate a menu system that allows you to define
   encrypted disk areas (NDisks). You can also use this
   menu system to define encryption options such as selecting an encryption algorithm, wiping original files, or setting a session password.

■ You must supply a password to open an NDisk (stored by
   DISKREET as a hidden file on the physical disk) as a logical drive, but you do not have to supply the password for
   files stored in an open NDisk.

Caution: *Do not forget passwords you use to encrypt files
or set up NDisks. You cannot discover the correct password
if you forget it (not even with DISKEDIT).*

DISKTOOL

Description:

Provides six procedures that you can use to perform the following recovery and protection operations:

- Make a disk bootable

- Undo work done by the DOS RECOVER command

- Attempt to revive a defective diskette without destroying any data

- Mark a cluster usable or defective

- Save hard disk partition tables, boot records, and CMOS values to a floppy disk

- Restore hard disk partition tables, boot records, and CMOS values from a floppy disk

Syntax:

5.0   DISKTOOL

Parameters:

No parameters exist for the DISKTOOL utility. When you enter the DISKTOOL command at the MS-DOS prompt or select DISKTOOL from the NORTON menu, a main menu presents selections for each of the functions described above. See Notes below for comments about each of the functions.

Notes:

- "Make a disk bootable" copies the system files COM-MAND.COM and MSDOS.SYS to the required locations, moving other files as necessary. This option creates a boot disk even in cases where the MS-DOS SYS command would produce the "No room for system files" error; it can also reconstruct the boot records on a disk and reconstruct the partition table.

- The "Recover from DOS's RECOVER" option attempts to restore a disk to the state it was in before you executed the MS-DOS RECOVER command. Use the Norton

Utilities NDD and UNERASE to restore a disk; you should never use the MS-DOS RECOVER command to attempt to restore a disk that has bad sectors or a bad directory structure. Unlike the MS-DOS RECOVER command, the Norton Utilities NDD and UNERASE preserve any subdirectories and the file entries in them. If you have used the IMAGE utility, chances are good that you can use NDD, UNERASE, and DISKEDIT to restore your disk completely. If you used the MS-DOS RECOVER command before using the Norton Utilities, you can repair the damage done by recover with this option.

■ Use "Revive a Defective Diskette" when you receive read errors such as "sector not found" on a floppy diskette. This option writes new physical format information to a diskette without destroying the data on the diskette.

■ The "Mark a Cluster" option allows you to mark physical clusters on a disk as usable or unusable. This option disables clusters that fail intermittently and moves data out of those clusters.

■ Use "Create Rescue Diskette" to copy critical information about your hard disk's boot records, partition tables, and CMOS values to a floppy disk. Use the "Restore Rescue Diskette" option to copy this information back to your hard disk from a previous rescue copy if the disk fails and you cannot recover it with NDD.

See also: DISKEDIT, IMAGE, NDD, UNERASE.

DP (Data Protect)

Description:
Saves information about selected files in a file named FRECOVER.DAT. The NU, QU, or UD utility can later use that information to recover lost data quickly and accurately.

Syntax:

4.5   DP [*drive*:]

5.0   *See* IMAGE

Parameter:

drive: The single-letter designator for the drive you want to process. Follow the letter with a colon. The current drive is the default.

Notes:

■   Include a DP command in your AUTOEXEC.BAT file to provide maximum protection for your system hard disk.

■   You cannot recover lost data on a floppy disk that has been reformatted using the MS-DOS FORMAT command. Use the Norton SF (Safe Format) utility instead.

■   DP is available only in version 4.5. In version 5.0, DP is incorporated into the IMAGE command.

See also: IMAGE, NU, QU, SF, UD.

DS (Directory Sort)

Description:

Sorts entries in a directory and can also sort entries in all subdirectories.

Syntax:

3.0, 3.1   DS *sort-order* [*path*] [/S]

4.0   DS *sort-order* [*path*] [/S]

DS [*path*] [/D0 | /D1 | D2][[[/F*n*] [/B*n*]] | /BW | /TV]

4.5   DS *sort-order* [*path*] [/S]

DS [*path*] [/D0 | /D1] [/BW] [/NOSNOW]

5.0   *See* SPEEDISK (See first item under Notes.)

Parameters:

sort-order One or more characters that define the order and
sequence by which you want to sort the current or specified
directory path. Type the character N for filename, E for file
extension, D for create date, T for create time, and S for file
size, concatenating the characters in the order in which you
want to sort the directory entries. In versions 3.1 and later,
follow any character in *sort-order* with a minus-sign character (−) to sort in descending sequence. If you do not provide
sort-order in versions 4.0 and 4.5, DS displays a full-screen
menu that you use to define the sort order. See Notes below
for information about how to use the menu.

path The fully qualified name of the directory you want to
sort. The current directory is the default.

/B*n* In version 4.0 specifies the background color for the
menu if you do not specify *sort-order*. Use an integer from
0 through 15 to specify the color. If you attempt to specify
identical foreground and background colors, DS adds 1 to
the foreground color number before beginning execution.
Avoid using the high-intensity shade of a color for the foreground with the normal-intensity shade of the same color for
the background (for example, /F12 bright red and /B4 red).
The default is /B1 (blue). See Appendix D.

/BW Specifies a black-and-white display.

/D0 In versions 4.0 and 4.5, requests the standard screen
driver (the default) for a fully IBM-compatible computer
system.

/D1 In versions 4.0 and 4.5, requests the screen driver for a
BIOS-compatible computer system.

/D2 In version 4.0, requests the ANSI.SYS driver for a non-
IBM-compatible computer system.

/F*n* In version 4.0, specifies the foreground color for the
menu if you do not specify *sort-order*. Use an integer from
0 through 15 to specify the color. The default is /F15 (bright
white). See Appendix D.

/NOSNOW Prevents screen flicker if your system has an older CGA card.

/S Sorts all files in all subdirectories under the specified path. In versions 4.0 and 4.5, DS ignores this switch if you do not specify *sort-order*.

/TV Indicates that the utility is running under either Top-View or Microsoft Windows.

Notes:

■ If you have version 4.5 installed prior to upgrading to version 5.0, the version 5.0 Install program allows you to copy this utility into the 5.0 subdirectory so that you can continue to use it with the new version.

■ DS is incorporated into the SPEEDISK command in version 5.0.

■ If you turn off your computer while DS is sorting entries, you might damage your directory.

■ DS places the sorted subdirectory entries ahead of sorted file entries in the target directory. In versions 4.0 and later, use the menu mode to alter this sequence.

■ Figure 1 shows a sample directory sort menu for versions 4.0 and 4.5. To specify the sort order, first press either the Tab key or the letter C to move the cursor to the right side of the menu. Then type the letter N, E, D, T, or S to choose the sort order. Type a minus-sign character (−) after any letter to indicate descending sequence. In the figure below, an ascending sort by Extension and within Extension by Size has been chosen. Press R to sort the entries using the sort criteria on the right.

You can also resequence individual entries. From the left side of the menu, use the arrow keys and the Spacebar to select the individual entries you want to move. In the example, two entries have been marked. Press M to begin the move and the Enter key to complete the move. Press W to write the changes to disk. Exit the menu by pressing either F10 or Escape.

```
┌─────────────────────── Directory Sort ───────────────────────┐
│            C:\UTILITY\NORTON                                  │
│     Name       Size      Date      Time                      │
│  SAMPLES1      <DIR>    Sep 17 89   9:10 am    Sort by    Order│
│  SAMPLES2      <DIR>    Sep 17 89   9:10 am                   │
│ ▶read    me      5,553  Jan  3 89   4:51 pm    Extension    + │
│  ds      exe    36,304  Jan  3 89   4:51 pm    Size        + │
│  dt      exe    21,328  Jan  3 89   4:51 pm                   │
│  ff      exe     9,042  Jan  3 89   4:51 pm                   │
│  fr      exe    44,670  Jan  3 89   4:51 pm                   │
│  ndd     exe   122,286  Jan  3 89   4:51 pm                   │
│  nu      exe   141,178  Jan  3 89   4:51 pm                   │
│ ▶nu      hlp    10,919  Jan  3 89   4:51 pm                   │
│  ncd     exe    36,136  Jan  3 89   4:51 pm        Name       │
│  ni      exe    42,972  Jan  3 89   4:51 pm        Extension  │
│  qu      exe    18,686  Jan  3 89   4:51 pm        Date       │
│  sd      exe    67,100  Jan  3 89   4:51 pm        Time       │
│  sf      exe    50,896  Jan  3 89   4:51 pm        Size       │
│  ud      exe    19,660  Jan  3 89   4:51 pm                   │
│  be      exe    22,652  Jan  3 89   4:51 pm    Clear sort order│
│                                                Move sort entry│
│       Space bar selects files for moving                     │
│                                                              │
│  Re-sort     Move file(s)     Change sort order   Write changes to disk│
└────────────────────── Press F1 for Help ─────────────────────┘
```

Figure 1. *Directory Sort menu—versions 4.0 and 4.5.*

Example:

To sort the directory \UTILITY\NORTON and all its subdirectories by file extension and by size, enter

```
DS ES \utility\norton /S
```

See also: LD, NCD, Appendix D.

DT (Disk Test)

Description:

Checks a disk for physical damage. In versions 4.0 and later,
you can mark a cluster as either usable or unusable, check
only a specific path, or attempt to move data that is stored in
bad clusters to a new area.

Syntax:

3.0   DT [*drive:*] [/F I /D I /B]

3.1   DT [*drive:*] [/F I /D I /B] [/LOG]

4.0, 4.5 DT [*drive*:][[*path* [/S]] | [/F | /D | /B]] [/C*n*[-] ...]

DT [*drive*:][*path*]*filename*

5.0 *See* DISKTOOL, NDD

Parameters:

drive: The single-letter designator for the drive you want to test. Follow the letter with a colon. The current drive is the default.

path The fully qualified name of the directory that contains the files whose clusters you want to test. If you include either the /B or the /D switch with this parameter, *path* is ignored, and DT tests the entire disk and all files on it.

filename The name of the file or files whose clusters you want to test. If you include either the /B or the /D switch with this parameter, *filename* is ignored and DT tests the entire disk and all files on it. The default *filename* is *.*.

/B Tests the entire disk (/D) and all files on it (/F).

/C*n*– Marks cluster *n* as usable.

/C*n* Marks cluster *n* as unusable.

/D Tests the entire disk, including system areas and unallocated areas.

/F Tests all allocated file areas on the disk.

/LOG Writes diagnostic output as separate (not overlaid) output lines; you can send the output to a printer or a disk file by including the MS-DOS redirection character (>) followed by a printer name or a filename at the end of the command.

/M Attempts to move data stored in unreadable clusters to a new location and marks the clusters as unreadable.

/S Tests all files in all subdirectories under the current or specified path.

Notes:

- You can stop the disk test at any time by pressing Ctrl-C or Ctrl-Break.

- DT is incorporated into the NDD command in version 5.0.

Example:

To test the GAMES directory on drive B, to move data stored in unreadable clusters to a new location, and to write the output diagnostics to the file *test.log*, enter

```
DT b:\games /M /LOG > test.log
```

FA (File Attributes)

Description:

Searches for files and displays file attributes. This command can also set and clear file attributes.

Syntax:

3.0   FA [*drive*:][*path*][*filename*] [/A[+|-]] [/R[+|-]] [/P] [/T] [/U]

3.1   FA [*drive*:][*path*][*filename*] [/A[+|-]] [/HID[+|-]] [/R[+|-]]
           [/SYS[+|-]] [/P] [/S] [/T] [/U]

4.0, 4.5   FA [*drive*:][*path*][*filename*] [/A[+|-]] [/HID[+|-]]
                [/R[+|-]] [/SYS[+|-]] [/CLEAR] [/P] [/S] [/T] [/U]

5.0   *See* FILEFIND (See first item under Notes.)

Parameters:

drive: The single-letter designator for the drive you want to search. Follow the letter with a colon. The current drive is the default.

path The fully qualified name of the directory you want to search. The current directory for the designated drive is the default.

filename The name of the file for which you want to search. The default *filename* is *.*.

/A Searches only for files with the archive attribute.

/A+ Sets (turns on) the archive attribute on all files whose names match *drive:\path\filename.*

/A− Clears (turns off) the archive attribute on all files with the archive attribute set and whose names match *drive:\path\filename.*

/CLEAR Clears (turns off) all file attributes on all files whose names match *drive:\path\filename.*

/HID Searches only for files with the hidden attribute.

/HID+ Sets (turns on) the hidden attribute on all files whose names match *drive:\path\filename.*

/HID− Clears (turns off) the hidden attribute on all hidden files whose names match *drive:\path\filename.*

/P Displays the results in pause mode: You initially see one screenful of information, and you must press a key to see each subsequent screenful.

Versions 3.0 and 3.1 Press any key to see the next screenful. Press the Pause key to pause at any time. You cannot activate pause mode after FA begins executing. Use Ctrl-C or Ctrl-Break to stop execution.

Versions 4.0 and 4.5 Press the Spacebar to see the next screenful. Press the Enter key to scroll up one line at a time. Press any key other than Spacebar, Enter, or Escape to leave pause mode. You can also enter pause mode during normal display by pressing any key other than Escape. Use the Escape key to stop execution.

/R Searches only for files with the read-only attribute.

/R+ Sets (turns on) the read-only attribute on all files whose names match *drive:\path\filename.*

/R− Resets (turns off) the read-only attribute on all files that are marked read-only and whose names match *drive:\path\filename.*

/S Searches all files in all subdirectories under the current or specified path.

/SYS Searches only for files with the system attribute.

/SYS+ Sets (turns on) the system attribute on all files whose names match *drive:\path\filename*.

/SYS– Resets (turns off) the system attribute on all system files whose names match *drive:\path\filename*.

/T Displays the total number of files whose attributes FA has changed. FA displays a total for each directory. If FA is in pause mode (see /P), the utility might pause several times before you see a total.

/U Displays all unusual files; that is, those with any of the four file attributes set.

Notes:

■ If you have version 4.5 installed prior to upgrading to version 5.0, the version 5.0 Install program allows you to copy this utility into the 5.0 subdirectory so that you can continue to use it with the new version.

■ FA is incorporated into the FILEFIND command in version 5.0.

Example:

To reset the read-only attribute on all files in the GAMES\ADVENT directory on the current drive and to display the names of all files that have the archive, the system, or the hidden attribute, enter

```
FA \games\advent /R- /U
```

See also: FF, FI, FILEFIND, FS, LD, NCD.

FD (File Date)

Description:

Sets or clears the date stamp or time stamp or both on selected files.

Syntax:

4.5   FD [*drive*:][*path*][*filename*] [/D*date*] [/T*time*] [/S] [/P]

5.0   *See* FILEFIND (See first item under Notes.)

Parameters:

drive: The single-letter designator for the drive you want to use. Follow the letter with a colon. The current drive is the default.

path The fully qualified name of the directory you want to process. The current directory for the designated drive is the default.

filename The name of the file whose date stamp or time stamp you want to set or clear. The default *filename* is *.*.

/D*date* The date value you want to set in the selected files. Specify *date* in the form [*mm*-[*dd*[-*yy*]]] if COUNTRY=01 (USA) in your CONFIG.SYS file. You must enter (-) dashes to separate *mm*, *dd*, and *yy*. If you supply the /D switch with no date value, FD resets the date on the selected files to 00-00-80. If you supply neither the /D nor the /T parameter, FD uses the current date. If you supply only a /D value, FD does not change the time on the file. If you specify *mm*-, FD sets the *dd* and the *yy* to 00. If you specify only *mm*-*dd*, FD sets *yy* to 00. Acceptable values are

mm = 01–12

dd = 01–31

yy = 00–99

Note that FD does not check to ensure that *dd* is valid for a specific month.

/P Displays the results in pause mode: You initially see one screenful of information, and you must press the Spacebar to see each subsequent screenful. Press Enter to scroll up one line at a time. Press any key other than Spacebar, Enter, or Escape to leave pause mode. You can also enter pause mode during normal display by pressing any key other than Escape. Use the Escape key to stop execution.

/S Processes all files in all subdirectories under the current or specified path.

/T*time* The time value you want to set in the selected files. Specify *time* in the form [*hh*[*:mm*[*:ss*]]], using colons (:) to separate *hh*, *mm*, and *ss*. If you supply /T with no time value, FD resets the time on the selected files to 12:00:00. If you supply neither the /D nor the /T parameter, FD uses the current time. If you supply only a /T value, FD does not change the date on the file. Acceptable values are

hh = 0–23

mm = 0–59

ss = 0–59

Notes:

■ If you have version 4.5 installed prior to upgrading to version 5.0, the version 5.0 Install program allows you to copy this utility into the 5.0 subdirectory so that you can continue to use it with the new version.

■ FD is incorporated into the FILEFIND command in version 5.0.

Example:

To reset the date to 9/4/82 and the time to 2:00 P.M. on all EXE files in the GAMES directory on drive B, enter

```
FD b:\games\*.exe /D09-04-82 /T14
```

See also: FA, FF, FI, FS, LD, NCD.

FF (File Find)

Description:

Searches either all drives or selected drives and finds and displays all files and directories whose names match the *filename* you specify.

Syntax:

3.0   FF [*drive*:...] [*filename*] [/P] [/W]

3.1, 4.0, 4.5   FF [*drive*:][*filename*] [*drive*:]...] [/A] [/P] [/W]

5.0   *See* FILEFIND (See first item under Notes.)

FL [*drive*:][*filename*] [*drive*:]...] [/A] [/P] [/W]

Parameters:

drive: The single-letter designator for the drive or drives you want to search. Follow each letter with a colon. The current drive is the default.

filename The name of the file for which you want to search. If you do not specify *filename*, FF lists all files and directories on the specified drive or drives; the default is *.*. If you specify one or more *drive*: values after *filename*, FF also searches those drives for *filename*.

/A Searches all drives. If a drive can't be accessed, FF skips it and does not display an error message.

/P Displays the results in pause mode: You initially see one screenful of information, and you must press a key to see each subsequent screenful.

Versions 3.0 and 3.1 Press any key to see the next screenful. Press the Pause key to pause at any time. You cannot activate pause mode after FF begins executing. Use Ctrl-C or Ctrl-Break to stop execution.

Versions 4.0, 4.5, and 5.0 Press the Spacebar to see the next screenful. Press the Enter key to scroll up one line at a time. Press any key other than Spacebar, Enter, or Escape to leave pause mode. You can also enter pause mode during normal display by pressing any key other than Escape. Use the Escape key to stop execution.

/W   Lists the files and directories in wide format (five files per line).

Notes:

■ If you have version 4.5 installed prior to upgrading to version 5.0, the version 5.0 Install program allows you to copy this utility into the 5.0 subdirectory and rename it FL so that you can continue to use it with the new version.

■ FF is incorporated into the FILEFIND command in version 5.0.

Example:

To search all drives and display all EXE files that begin with the letters WIN, enter

```
FF win*.exe /A
```

See also: FA, FI, FILEFIND, FS, LD, NCD.

FI (File Info)

Description:

Either saves comments about files or lists specified directories and the file comments saved previously with this command. FI saves comments about files in a file named FILEINFO.FI in each specified directory. If FILEINFO.FI does not exist, FI creates it.

Syntax:

4.0   FI [*drive*:][*path*][*filename*] [*comment*] [/C] [/D] [/E] [/L] [/N] [/P] [/PACK] [/S]

4.5   FI [*drive*:][*path*][*filename*] [*comment*] [/C] [/D] [/E] [/L] [/P] [/PACK] [/S]

5.0 *No equivalent*

Parameters:

drive: The single-letter designator for the drive you want
to use. Follow the letter with a colon. The current drive is
the default.

path The fully qualified name of the directory you want to
process. The current directory for the designated drive is
the default.

filename The name of the file whose FILEINFO.FI file
entry you want to update or list.

comment The comment you want to save with the specified
files. The comment can be a maximum of 65 characters long
and need not be enclosed in quotation marks.

/C Lists only those files that have comments.

/D Deletes comments from the specified files.

/E Lets you change or enter a comment in an edit window.
You can use WordStar-compatible editing commands within
the one-line edit window.

/L Displays the entire 65-character comment for each file. If
you include this switch, FI does not display the size, the date
stamp, and the time stamp of each file. If you omit /L, FI displays the file size, the date stamp, the time stamp, and the
first 36 characters of each stored comment.

/N Use this switch with the /E switch if your machine is not
fully IBM-compatible.

/P Displays the results in pause mode: You initially see one
screenful of information, and you must press the Spacebar to
see the next screenful. Press Enter to scroll up one line at a
time. Press any key other than Spacebar, Enter, or Escape to
leave pause mode. You can also enter pause mode during
normal display by pressing any key other than Escape. Use
the Escape key to stop execution.

/PACK Compresses deleted (flagged but not removed) entries from the FILEINFO.FI file.

/S Processes all files in all subdirectories under the current or specified path.

Example:

To add the comment "Microsoft Word Document" to all DOC files in the NORTBOOK directory and its subdirectories and to display the results in pause mode, enter

```
FI \nortbook\*.DOC Microsoft Word Document /P /S
```

See also: FA, FF, FS, LD, NCD.

FILEFIND

Description:

Locates files by name, by content, or both; alters file attributes and dates.

Syntax:

5.0 FILEFIND [*drive*:][*path*][*filename*] [*text*] [/A[+|-]]
[/BATCH] [/C] [/CLEAR] [/CS] [/D[*date*]] [/HID[+|-]]
[/NOW] [/O:[*outdrive*:][*outpath*]*outfile*] [/R[+|-]] [/S]
[/SYS[+|-]] [/T[*time*]] [/TARGET:*todrive*]

Parameters:

drive: The single-letter designator for the drive you want to search. Follow the letter with a colon. The current drive is the default. Use the special character * in this position to search all drives.

path The name of the path you want FILEFIND to consider the current path. The current directory for the specified *drive* is the default. If you specify a *path*, you must also specify a *filename*.

filename The name of the file for which you want to search.
The default is *.*, which in the absence of a *drive* or *path*
tells FILEFIND to search the entire current drive.

FILEFIND recognizes the special filenames .*.* (search all
files on the current directory) and *:*.* (search all files on
all drives).

text A text string for which you want to search. If the text
string is more than a single word, you must enclose it in quotation marks. If the text string contains a single quotation
mark character, enclose the text in double quotation marks.
If the text contains a double quotation mark character, enclose the text in single quotation marks. FILEFIND matches
either lowercase or uppercase letters unless you specify the
/CS switch (that is, "A" is the same as "a").

/A Searches only for files with the archive attribute.

/A+ Sets (turns on) the archive attribute on all files whose
names match *drive*:*path**filename*.

/A− Clears (turns off) the archive attribute on all files with
the archive attribute set and whose names match
drive:*path**filename*.

/BATCH Terminates FILEFIND after all command line
parameters are honored. Use this switch when executing
FILEFIND from a batch file.

/C Searches the current directory (identical to specifying a
filename of .*.*).

/CLEAR Clears (turns off) all file attributes on all files
whose names match *drive*:*path**filename*.

/CS Performs a case-sensitive search for *text*.

/D[*date*] Sets the date value to *date* in the selected files.
Specify *date* in the form *mm-dd-yy* if COUNTRY=01 (USA)
in your CONFIG.SYS file. You must enter dashes (-) to
separate *mm*, *dd*, and *yy*. If you supply the /D switch with no
date value, FILEFIND resets the date on the selected files to
00-00-80. If you supply only a /D value, FILEFIND does not

change the time on the file. If you specify *mm-*, FILEFIND
sets the *dd* and the *yy* to 00. If you specify only *mm-dd*, FD
sets *yy* to 00. Acceptable values are

mm = 01–12

dd = 01–31

yy = 00–99

FILEFIND does not check to ensure that *dd* is valid for a specific month. In early copies of version 5.0, FILEFIND ignores values specified with the /D switch and sets the date to
00-00-80. To reset the file date to a specific value, use the
Set Date/Time dialog box by choosing Set Date/Time from
the Commands menu (available when FILEFIND is active).
See Figure 2 on page 53 for an illustration of the FILEFIND
dialog box and menu.

/HID Searches only for files with the hidden attribute.

/HID+ Sets (turns on) the hidden attribute on all files whose
names match *drive:\path\filename*.

/HID– Clears (turns off) the hidden attribute on all hidden
files whose names match *drive:\path\filename*.

/NOW Changes the date and time on the selected files to the
current date and time.

/O:[*outdrive:*][*outpath*]*outfile* Specifies a file to receive
the found file listing. When you include the /O switch,
FILEFIND automatically writes the name of the found files
to the specified file. If the file does not exist, FILEFIND
creates it. If the file does exist, FILEFIND prompts you for
permission to overwrite or append to the file. The filename
you specify also becomes the default filename for the
options in the List menu. If you do not specify this switch,
the default output filename for options in the List menu is
FILELIST.BAT.

/R Searches only for files with the read-only attribute.

/R+ Sets (turns on) the read-only attribute on all files whose
names match *drive:\path\filename*.

/R– Resets (turns off) the read-only attribute on all files that are marked read-only and whose names match *drive:\path\filename*.

/S Searches all files in all subdirectories under the current or specified path.

/SYS Searches only for files with the system attribute.

/SYS+ Sets (turns on) the system attribute on all files whose names match *drive:\path\filename*.

/SYS– Resets (turns off) the system attribute on all system files whose names match *drive:\path\filename*.

/T[*time*] Sets the time value to *time* in the selected files. Specify *time* in the form *hh:mm[:ss]* using colons (:) to separate *hh*, *mm*, and *ss*. If you supply the /T switch with no time value, FILEFIND resets the time on the selected files to 12:00:00. If you supply only a /T value, FILEFIND does not change the date on the file. Acceptable values are

hh = 0–23

mm = 0–59

ss = 0–59

In early copies of version 5.0, FILEFIND ignores the /T switch. To reset the file time, use the set Date/Time dialog box by choosing set Date/Time from the Commands menu.

/TARGET:*todrive* Determines whether the specified drive contains enough space in which to copy the selected files.

Notes:

■ When you install Norton Utilities Version 5.0, you can give FILEFIND the short name of FF. In the syntax line above, use FF instead of FILEFIND if you selected this option.

■ When you execute FILEFIND with no parameters, you can use the dialog box and menu (see Figure 2) to select search parameters (Search), alter file attributes

(Commands), or produce an output report or batch file
(List). Select Start to begin a search, and View to view
the contents of selected files.

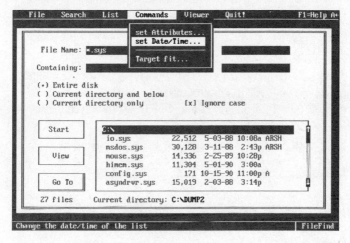

Figure 2. *FILEFIND dialog box and menu.*

- Use DISKEDIT to search for characters that you cannot enter in *text* from the keyboard.

- You can use the following shortcut key combinations in the FILEFIND menu system:

Key	Function
Alt-D	Select drives to search
Ctrl-B	Create a batch file using the list
Ctrl-D	Change current drive
Ctrl-F	Select list display and sort options
Ctrl-P	Print the list to a printer or file and select list format options
Ctrl-R	Change current directory
F4	Specify advanced search (search by date, size, owner, or attributes)
F5	In View option, show previous *text* match
F6	In View option, show next *text* match

(continued)

(continued)

Key	Function
F7	In View option, show contents of previous file
F8	In View option, show contents of next file

Example:

To search for all occurrences of "data base" in all files with the extension TXT in all directories in drive C, determine if these files will fit on drive D, and produce an output list to file C:\DATA\TEXT.LST, enter

```
FILEFIND C:\*.TXT /S /TARGET:D /O:C:\DATA\TEXT.LST
```

See also: DISKEDIT, FA, FD, FS, NORTON, TS.

FILEFIX

Description:
Repairs damaged Lotus 1-2-3, Symphony, dBASE, FoxBase, or Clipper files.

Syntax:
5.0 FILEFIX [*drive*:][*path*][*filename*]

Parameters:

drive: The single-letter designator for the drive you want to process. Follow the letter with a colon. The current drive is the default.

path The fully qualified name of the directory you want to process. The current directory for the designated drive is the default.

filename The name of the file you want to fix. You can use the wildcard characters * and ? to perform a search. When you include a DBF, WR*, or WK* file extension, FILEFIX

automatically enters the appropriate recovery mode for the
file type. Otherwise, FILEFIX first prompts you for the type
of file you want to recover before it begins a search.

Notes:

■ You may need to execute UNERASE first to restore deleted dBASE, Lotus 1-2-3, or Symphony files before
using FILEFIX to recover their contents.

■ FILEFIX allows you to recover files to a different
filename on a different drive. Use this option when you
might have to make more than one attempt to recover the
data in a badly damaged file. The default *filename*
FILEFIX generates is FIXED.WK1 (or WR1 or DBF) on
the current drive; change the default filename to recover
files to another filename or drive.

■ When restoring Lotus 1-2-3 or Symphony files, use the
Attempt recovery of all data option first. If this fails,
FILEFIX can usually recover at least the cell data.

■ For dBASE files, FILEFIX provides you with a compre-
hensive menu facility to restore the data and file structure
of badly damaged (or zapped) dBASE files. Even if part
of the file structure definition is lost (normally stored in
the dBASE file header), you can rebuild it using FILEFIX.

See also: DISKEDIT, UNERASE.

FILESAVE

Description:

Provides added protection against inadvertent deletion of important files by moving them to a special hidden directory at
the end of the disk when you delete them. (The hidden directory is named TRASHCAN.) You can specify which drives
and files to protect and when to permanently delete files.

Syntax:

5.0   FILESAVE [/<u>STAT</u>US | /ON | [/OFF | /<u>UN</u>INSTALL]]

Parameters:

/ON   Installs FILESAVE as a terminate-and-stay-resident
(TSR) program to protect files being deleted.

/OFF   Removes FILESAVE from memory and turns off file
protection.

/<u>STAT</u>US   Displays the current FILESAVE install status
and protection options.

/<u>UN</u>INSTALL   Same as /OFF.

Notes:

- Enter FILESAVE without any parameters to establish
  which files are to be saved, the limit for the amount of
  data saved, and the number of days that files are saved.
  FILESAVE stores protection parameters in the file
  FILESAVE.INI.

- You can also use FILESAVE to manually purge file
  copies that are being saved.

- Use UNERASE to restore deleted files captured by
  FILESAVE.

See also: DISKEDIT, UNERASE.

FR (Format Recover)

Description:

In the Advanced Edition of versions 4.0 and 4.5, either saves
information about all files on a disk you specify or recovers
from an inadvertent use of the MS-DOS FORMAT command or RECOVER command by restoring file information.

Syntax:

4.0   FR [*drive:*] [/SAVE] [/D0 | /D1 | /D2] [[[/F*n*] [/B*n*]] | /BW | /TV]

4.5   FR [*drive*:] [/SAVE] [/NOBAK] [/D0 | /D1] [/BW]
       [/NOSNOW]

5.0   *See* UNFORMAT

Parameters:

drive: The single-letter designator for the drive you want
to use. Follow the letter with a colon. If you include the
/SAVE switch and do not specify a drive, FR processes the
current drive.

/B*n* Specifies the background color for the menu system in
version 4.0 if you do not provide the /SAVE switch. Use an
integer from 0 through 15 to specify the color. If you attempt
to specify identical foreground and background colors, FR
adds 1 to the foreground color number before beginning execution. Avoid using the high-intensity shade of a color for
the foreground with the normal-intensity shade of the same
color for the background (for example, /F12 bright red and
/B4 red). The default is /B1 (blue). See Appendix D.

/BW Specifies a black-and-white display.

/D0 Requests the standard screen driver (the default) for a
fully IBM-compatible computer system.

/D1 Requests the screen driver for a BIOS-compatible computer system.

/D2 Requests the ANSI.SYS driver for a non-IBM-
compatible computer system.

/F*n* Specifies the foreground color for the menu system in
version 4.0 if you do not provide the /SAVE switch. Use an
integer from 0 through 15 to specify the color. The default is
/F15 (bright white). See Appendix D.

/NOSNOW Prevents screen flicker if your system has an
older CGA card.

/NOBAK If you either use the /SAVE switch or select the
Save menu option, this switch prevents FR from making a
backup copy of the existing FRECOVER.DAT file before
creating a current version of the file.

/SAVE Analyzes the disk and creates a FRECOVER.DAT
file that FR can use in a subsequent recover operation to rebuild the root directory, the file allocation table, and all directories. If you do not specify /SAVE, FR displays full-screen
menus you use to select both the command you want (either
Save or Recover) and the drive you want to process. See
Notes below. Note that some early releases of version 4.0 do
not include the menu system.

/TV Indicates that the utility is running under either
TopView or Microsoft Windows.

Notes:

- To provide maximum protection for your system
  hard disk, include an FR /SAVE command in your
  AUTOEXEC.BAT file.

- In version 4.0, you can use FR only with hard disks. In
  version 4.5, you can use FR with either a floppy disk or
  a hard disk.

- FR is incorporated into the UNFORMAT command in
  version 5.0.

- FR cannot recover data on a floppy disk that was
  reformatted using the MS-DOS FORMAT command. Instead, reformat using the Norton SF (Safe Format) utility,
  which is found in version 4.5. Also, FR cannot recover
  data on a floppy disk that was reformatted at a different
  density.

- The FRECOVER.DAT file created by the /SAVE option
  of FR in version 4.5 is not compatible with version 4.0.

- If you have not previously run FR with the /SAVE switch
  against a disk you are attempting to recover, FR cannot rebuild the root directory or the files that were in the root directory. If the files on the disk are badly fragmented, the
  file allocation table (FAT) might be incorrect. You can
  avoid disk fragmentation by periodically executing the
  SD (Speed Disk) utility, which is found in the Advanced
  Edition of versions 4.0 and 4.5.

- The menu system contains four main options:

    ☐ Restore information by attempting to locate a
       FRECOVER.DAT file.

    ☐ Unformat the disk by rebuilding the subdirectories and
       the files in them (because no FRECOVER.DAT file
       was created on the disk).

    ☐ Save disk information in a FRECOVER.DAT file.

    ☐ Exit.

    The menus also let you specify the drive you want to pro-
    cess. The Recover and Unformat options let you cancel
    the operation if any files currently exist on the target disk.
    Note that the MS-DOS RECOVER command creates
    dummy FILE*nnnn* entries and that FR can overwrite them.

- After you use FR to recover a disk, you might need to execute the MS-DOS CHKDSK command or run the Norton
  NDD (Norton Disk Doctor) utility (in version 4.5) to ensure that FR restored all files correctly.

See also: NDD, NU, QU, SD, SF, UD, UNFORMAT.

FS (File Size)

Description:

Displays the size of each selected file, the total size of all
selected files, and the percentage of allocated space used for
selected files within a directory or subdirectory. FS can also
determine whether the selected files will fit on a specified
target disk.

Syntax:

3.0   FS [*drive*:][*path*][*filename*] [*to-drive*:] [/P] [/T]

3.1, 4.0, 4.5   FS [*drive*:][*path*][*filename*] [*to-drive*:] [/P] [/S] [/T]

5.0   *See* FILEFIND (See first item under Notes.)

Parameters:

drive: The single-letter designator for the drive you want to search. Follow the letter with a colon. The current drive is the default.

path The fully qualified name of the directory you want to search. The current directory for the designated drive is the default.

filename The name of the file for which you want to search. The default *filename* is *.*.

to-drive: The single-letter designator for the drive you want to check to determine whether the drive contains enough space in which to copy the selected files. Follow the letter with a colon.

/P Displays the results in pause mode: You initially see one screenful of information, and you must press a key to see each subsequent screenful.

Versions 3.0 and 3.1 Press any key to see the next screenful. Press the Pause key to pause at any time. You cannot activate pause mode after FS begins executing. Use Ctrl-C or Ctrl-Break to stop execution.

Versions 4.0 and 4.5 Press the Spacebar to see the next screenful. Press the Enter key to scroll up one line at a time. Press any key other than Spacebar, Enter, or Escape to leave pause mode. You can also enter pause mode during normal display by pressing any key other than Escape. Use the Escape key to stop execution.

/S Processes all files in all subdirectories under the current or specified path.

/T Displays the total space statistics for selected files. FS displays a total for each directory. If FS is in pause mode (see /P), the utility might pause several times before you see a total.

Notes:

■ If you have version 4.5 installed prior to upgrading to version 5.0, the version 5.0 Install program allows you to copy this utility into the 5.0 subdirectory so that you can continue to use it with the new version.

■ FS is incorporated into the FILEFIND command in version 5.0

Example:

To determine the file sizes of all EXE files in the GAMES directory and all subdirectories on the current drive and to determine whether the selected files and all subdirectories will fit on the disk in drive B, enter

```
FS \games\*.exe b: /S
```

See also: FA, FF, FI, FILEFIND, LD, NCD.

IMAGE

Description:

Saves information about selected files in a file named IMAGE.DAT. The UNERASE and UNFORMAT utilities can later use that information to recover lost data more quickly and accurately.

Syntax:

5.0   IMAGE [*drive*:]... [/NOBACKUP]

Parameters:

drive: The single-letter designator for the drive you want to process. Follow the letter with a colon. The current drive is the default. Specify additional *drive:* parameters to process multiple drives.

/NOBACKUP Specifies that you do not want the previous copy of IMAGE.DAT saved as IMAGE.BAK.

Notes:

■ Include an IMAGE command in your AUTOEXEC.BAT file to provide maximum protection for your system disks.

■ You cannot recover lost data on a floppy disk that has been reformatted using the MS-DOS FORMAT command. Use the Norton SFORMAT (Safe Format) utility instead.

■ The version 4.5 FRECOVER.DAT file is compatible with IMAGE.DAT. The first time you execute IMAGE, the utility renames any existing FRECOVER.DAT file IMAGE.DAT.

■ Because you may not discover a damaged system disk until you have booted your computer and successfully created a new IMAGE.DAT file, always allow IMAGE to create a backup copy (by not specifying the /NOBACKUP switch). You can then use the IMAGE.BAK file to restore your disk.

See also: SFORMAT, UNERASE, UNFORMAT.

LD (List Directories)

Description:

Displays the directory structure of selected drives. In versions 4.0 and later, you can specify a starting *path* and request a graphic display of its structure.

Syntax:

3.0   LD [*drive*:] [/P] [/W]

3.1   LD [*drive*:]... [/A] [/P] [/T I /W]

4.0, 4.5   LD [*drive*:][*path*] [*drive*:]...] [/A] [/G [/N] I /T] [/P]

5.0   *See* NCD

Parameters:

drive: The single-letter designator for the drive whose directory structure you want to display. Follow the letter with a
colon. The current drive is the default. In versions 3.1 and
later, you can provide multiple drive-designators to process
more than one drive.

path The fully qualified name of the directory you want
to display. The root directory for the designated drive is
the default.

/A Displays the directories on all drives. If a drive can't be
accessed, LD skips it and does not display an error message.

/G Displays the directories in a graphic tree structure.

/N If you include the /G switch, LD uses standard characters
instead of extended graphic characters to draw the tree structure. Use the /N switch if you want to direct the output to a
device that does not support the extended character set.

/P Displays the results in pause mode: You initially see one
screenful of information, and you must press a key to see
each subsequent screenful.

Versions 3.0 and 3.1 Press any key to see the next screenful. Press the Pause key to pause at any time. You cannot activate pause mode after LD begins executing. Use Ctrl-C or
Ctrl-Break to stop execution.

Versions 4.0 and 4.5 Press the Spacebar to see the next
screenful. Press the Enter key to scroll up one line at a time.
Press any key other than Spacebar, Enter, or Escape to leave
pause mode. You can also enter pause mode during normal
display by pressing any key other than Escape. Use the Escape key to stop execution.

/T Displays the total number of files. LD displays a total
for each directory. This switch has no effect if you specify
either the /G switch or the /W switch. If LD is in pause mode
(see /P), the utility might pause several times before you see
a total.

/W Lists the files and directories in wide format (five
entries per line).

Note:

■ LD is incorporated into the NCD command in
version 5.0.

Example:

To print a graphic tree structure of all directories on all
drives, enter

```
LD /A /G > prn
```

See also: FA, FF, FI, FS, NCD.

LP (Line Print)

Description:

Prints a selected text file and provides options to let you control the format of the output.

Syntax:

3.0   LP [*drive*:][*path*]*filename*[[PRN | COM*n* | LPT*n*] |
        [*drive*:][*path*]*filename*] [/B*n*] [/H*n*] [/L*n*] [/N] [/P*n*] [/R*n*]
        [/S*n*] [/T*n*] [/W*n*] [/80 | /132]

3.1   LP [*drive*:][*path*]*filename* [[PRN | COM*n* | LPT*n*] |
        [*drive*:][*path*]*filename*] [/B*n*] [/EUR] [/H*n*] [/L*n*] [/N]
        [/NOH] [/P*n*] [/R*n*] [/S*n*] [/T*n*] [/W*n*] [/80 | /132]

4.0   LP [*drive*:][*path*]*filename* [[PRN[:] | COM*n*[:] | LPT*n*[:]] |
        [*drive*:][*path*]*filename*] [/B*n*] [/EBCDIC] [/EXT] [/H*n*]
        [/HEADER*n*] [/L*n*] [/N] [/P*n*] [/R*n*] [/S*n*]
        [/SET:[*drive*:][*path*]*filename*][/T*n*] [/W*n*] [/80 | /132]

4.5   LP [*drive*:][*path*]*filename* [[PRN[:] | COM*n*[:] | LPT*n*[:]] |
        [*drive*:][*path*]*filename*] [/B*n*] [/EBCDIC] [/H*n*]
        [/HEADER*n*] [/L*n*] [/N] [/P*n*] [/R*n*] [/S*n*]
        [/SET:[*drive*:][*path*]*filename*] [/T*n*] [/W*n*] [/WS]
        [/80 | /132]

5.0   *No equivalent*   (See also first item under Notes.)

Parameters:

drive: The single-letter designator for the drive that contains the file you want to print, the output file, or the printer setup (/SET:) file. Follow the letter with a colon. The current drive is the default.

path The fully qualified name of the directory that contains the file you want to print, the output file, or the printer setup (/SET:) file. The current directory for the designated drive is the default.

filename The name of the file you want to print, the name of the file to which you want to direct the output, or the file that contains printer setup (/SET:) information. You cannot use the * and ? wildcard characters in either the output filename or the setup information filename. If the output file does not exist, LP creates it.

PRN | COM*n* **| LPT***n* The logical name of the device to which you want to direct the output. To complete the COM or LPT name, supply an integer value (such as 1) for *n*. The default is the standard printer device. Note that in versions 4.0 and 4.5, you can include a colon after PRN, COM*n*, and LPT*n*.

/B*n* Sets the bottom margin, in number of lines. The default value for *n* is 5.

/EBCDIC Indicates that the input file is in Extended Binary Coded Decimal Interchange Code format rather than in ASCII format.

/EUR In version 3.1, specifies the European character set and sends character codes 128 through 255 to the printer without alteration. If you do not use this switch, LP removes the high-order bit from all characters to restrict the output range of codes to 0 through 127.

/EXT In version 4.0, specifies the extended character set and prints all characters without modification. If you do not use this switch, LP removes the high-order bit from all characters to restrict the output range of codes to 0 through 127.

/Hn Sets the page height, in number of lines. The default value for *n* is 66.

/HEADERn Specifies the type of header. If you do not want a header, use /HEADER0. (/HEADER0 is the same as /NOH in version 3.1.) /HEADER1, the default, produces a header with the input filename, the current date and time, and page numbers. /HEADER2 produces a header with the input filename, the current date and time, page numbers, and the input file date and time.

/Ln Sets the left margin, in number of columns. The default value for *n* is 5.

/N Turns on line numbering. If you do not use this switch, LP does not print line numbers.

/NOH In version 3.1, suppresses page headers. If you do not include this switch, the utility produces a page header that contains *filename*, the current date and time, and page numbers.

/Pn Sets the first page number. The default value for *n* is 1.

/Rn Sets the right margin, in number of columns. The default value for *n* is 5.

/Sn Sets line spacing. The default value for *n* is 1.

/SET: Specifies the file that contains printer setup information. LP translates the data in this file and sends the data to the printer before printing begins. LP does not reset printer control information when the output is complete. To reestablish printer defaults, send a Reset command sequence to your printer after using LP with /SET:. See the example on the next page.

Note that in the printer setup file, you enter special control codes either as *nnn* (where *nnn* is the decimal number for the code you want to produce) or as *x* (where *x* is any character that produces a valid Ctrl-*x* sequence). LP translates these codes before sending them to the printer. LP sends all other characters exactly as you entered them, but it does not send carriage returns.

/T*n* Sets the top margin, in number of lines. The default
value for *n* is 3.

/W*n* Sets the width of the page, in number of columns. The
default value for *n* is 85.

/WS In a WordStar input file, removes the high-order bit
from all characters to restrict the output range of codes to 0
through 127. The default in version 4.5 is to send character
codes 128 through 255 to the printer without alteration.

/80 Switches to normal print mode, which is the default.

/132 Switches to compressed print mode.

Note:

■ If you have version 4.5 installed prior to upgrading to version 5.0, the version 5.0 Install program allows you to
copy this utility into the 5.0 subdirectory so that you can
continue to use it with the new version.

Example:

To use version 4.5 to create a file named DIRGRPH.TXT
containing a graphic list of all directories on all drives and
to print the result on a Hewlett-Packard LaserJet II printer
using the IBM-US character set and the line printer font,
enter

```
LD /A /G > dirgrph.txt
LP dirgrph.txt /H80 /SET:lpibmus.txt
LP blank.txt /SET:reset.txt
```

where LPIBMUS.TXT contains

\027(10U	(Set to IBM-US character set)
\027(s0t16.66h8.5V	(Set to line printer font)
\027&18D	(Set to eight lines per inch)

and RESET.TXT contains

\027E

and BLANK.TXT is an empty file.

In version 4.0, you must add the /EXT switch to the first LP
command. Do not include the preceding parenthetical comments in the file LPIBMUS.TXT.

NCACHE-F
(Fast Norton Disk Cache)

Description:

Speeds up data access by using the computer's memory to
store active blocks and satisfying program reads for those
blocks from memory (which is very fast) rather than disk
(which is very slow). NCACHE-F is usually faster than
NCACHE-S (see the description of NCACHE-S) because
it can

■ Anticipate the next data that a program will request (particularly for sequential reads)

■ Initiate writes to the disk and return immediate control to
  an application program instead of waiting for the write to
  complete

■ Allow the next read of data to begin before any preceding
  write must complete.

However, NCACHE-F requires significantly more memory
than NCACHE-S does, to remove stack.

Syntax:

5.0 In CONFIG.SYS:

    DEVICE=[drive:][path]NCACHE-F.EXE [/BLOCK=blksz]
        [/DELAY=ss[.hh]] [/DOS=[-]dosmem]
        [/EXT=[-]extmem] [/EXP=[-]expmem]
        [/QUICK={ON I OFF}] [/USEHIDOS={YES I NO}]
        [/USEHMA={YES I NO}] [[drive:] [{+I-}A] [{+I-}C]
        [G=grpsz] [{+I-}I] [R=[D]rdnum] [{+I-}S] [{+I-}W]]...

In AUTOEXEC.BAT:

NCACHE-F [/BLOCK=*blksz*] [/DELAY=*ss*[.*hh*]]
   [/DOS=[-]*dosmem*] [/EXT=[-]*extmem*]
   [/EXP=[-]*expmem*] [/QUICK={ON | OFF}]
   [/USEHIDOS={YES | NO}] [/USEHMA={YES | NO}]
   [[*drive:*] [{+|-}A] [{+|-}C] [G=*grpsz*] [{+|-}I]
   [R=[D]*rdnum*] [{+|-}S] [{+|-}W]]...

From the command line:

NCACHE-F [/BLOCK=*blksz*] [/DELAY=*ss*[.*hh*]]
   [/DOS=[-]*dosmem*] [/EXT=[-]*extmem*]
   [/EXP=[-]*expmem*] [/QUICK={ON | OFF}] [/RESET]
   [/STATUS] [/UNINSTALL] [/USEHIDOS={YES | NO}]
   [/USEHMA={YES | NO}] [[*drive:*] [{+|-}A] [{+|-}C] [F]
   [G=*grpsz*] [{+|-}I] [R=[D]*rdnum*] [{+|-}S] [{+|-}W]]...

Parameters:

drive: The single-letter designator for the drive that contains the NCACHE-F program or the drive you want to affect with switch settings. Follow the letter with a colon. The current drive is the default for the NCACHE-F program location, and all drives is the default for switch settings.

path The fully qualified name of the directory that contains the NCACHE-F program. The default is the root path for the drive specified.

+A Activates caching for the specified drive, which is the default.

−A Deactivates caching for the specified drive if NCACHE-F is already active. Does not activate caching for the specified drive when starting NCACHE-F for the first time.

/BLOCK=*blksz* Size of the data blocks in memory. You can include this parameter only the first time you invoke NCACHE-F. Valid values for *blksz* are 512, 1K, 2K, 4K, and 8K. Use a smaller *blksz* if most of your files are small or fragmented. In early copies of version 5.0, NCACHE-F does not accept the value 512.

+C Allow new data being read to be placed in memory cache for the specified drive, which is the default.

–C Do not place any new data being read into memory cache for the specified drive.

/DELAY=_ss_[._hh_] Maximum time, in seconds and hundredths of seconds, that NCACHE-F should delay writes to the disk. The default is 00.00, indicating no delay. If you include a delay value for a cache for a floppy drive, you must always wait the amount of time specified before you remove a floppy disk after a write operation.

/DOS=_dosmem_ Indicates the amount of MS-DOS memory (below 640 KB), in KB, that you want NCACHE-F to use for cache buffers. You can include this parameter only the first time you invoke NCACHE-F. If your machine has extended or expanded memory that NCACHE-F can use, NCACHE-F allocates no MS-DOS memory for cache buffers. If no extended or expanded memory is available, the default is 128 KB.

/DOS=-_dosmem_ Indicates the amount of MS-DOS memory (below 640 KB) that you want NCACHE-F to leave for other programs. You can include this parameter only the first time you invoke NCACHE-F. If your machine has available extended or expanded memory, the default is to leave as much MS-DOS memory as possible.

/EXT=_extmem_ Indicates the amount of extended memory, in KB, that you want to allow NCACHE-F to use. You can include this parameter only the first time you invoke NCACHE-F. The default is to use all available extended memory. If you run applications that use extended memory (such as Microsoft Windows), you should limit the amount of extended memory NCACHE-F consumes so that some is left for these applications. NCACHE-F ignores this parameter if /USEHMA=NO.

/EXT=-_extmem_ Indicates the amount of extended memory, in KB, that you want NCACHE-F to leave for other applications. You can include this parameter only the first time you invoke NCACHE-F. The default is to leave no extended memory unallocated.

/EXP=*expmem* Indicates the amount of expanded memory, in KB, that you want to allow NCACHE-F to use. You can include this parameter only the first time you invoke NCACHE-F. The default is to use all available expanded memory. If you run applications that use expanded memory (such as Microsoft Windows), you should limit the amount of expanded memory NCACHE-F consumes so that some is left for these applications.

/EXP=-*expmem* Indicates the amount of expanded memory, in KB, that you want NCACHE-F to leave for other applications. You can include this parameter only the first time you invoke NCACHE-F. The default is to leave no expanded memory unallocated.

/F Clears the cache buffers. NCACHE-F completes all pending writes and empties the cache memory.

G=*grpsz* Specifies the group sector size. Valid values are 1 through 128, and the default value is 128. A small number limits the number of sectors that can be placed into memory in a single read. A smaller number can improve performance for small random reads.

+I Enables intelligent writes for the specified drive and is the default. NCACHE-F returns control to the application after a write is started without waiting for the write to complete.

–I Disables intelligent writes for the specified drive.

/QUICK={ON | OFF} When intelligent write is enabled, ON instructs NCACHE-F to return to the MS-DOS prompt immediately when a program completes execution rather than waiting for all writes to complete. If you specify ON, remember to allow NCACHE-F to complete all writes before you remove a floppy disk or shut off the computer. OFF finishes all writes before returning to the MS-DOS prompt. OFF is the default.

R=[D]*rdnum* Specifies how many sectors NCACHE-F reads ahead for the specified drive. Including the letter D instructs NCACHE-F to read ahead only when it has

detected that reads are sequential. That is, NCACHE-F performs no read-ahead on the very first read, but will read
ahead if the very next read is for the next sector. Omitting
the D slows down random reads because this causes
NCACHE-F to read extra sectors on every read. Valid values for *rdnum* are 0 (which turns off read-ahead) through 15;
if you do not specify a value, NCACHE-F selects a value optimal for the type of hard drive you have. The upper limit for
rdnum varies according to the type of hard drive you have.

/RESET Resets cache statistics. See Figure 3 on page 74.

+S Enables *smart reads* for the specified drive. This allows
new read commands to be started without forcing any pending write commands to be completed. This is the default.

–S Disables *smart reads* for the specified drive.

/STATUS Displays the status screen (see Figure 3 on
page 74). If you have not installed NCACHE-F and specify
no option other than /STATUS, NCACHE-F installs itself
using default parameters.

/UNINSTALL Clears all cache buffers and removes
NCACHE-F from memory. You cannot uninstall NCACHE-F
if you loaded it as a device driver in CONFIG.SYS. Also,
NCACHE-F must be the last terminate-and-stay-resident
(TSR) program loaded into memory to be able to uninstall it.
You can use the –A parameter to disable NCACHE-F without
uninstalling it.

/USEHIDOS={YES | NO} YES allows NCACHE-F to use
high MS-DOS memory (above 640 KB) if it is available.
You can include this parameter only the first time you invoke NCACHE-F. If either extended or expanded memory is
available, the default is NO.

/USEHMA={YES | NO} YES (the default) allows
NCACHE-F to use extended memory. You can include this
parameter only the first time you invoke NCACHE-F. If you
encounter conflicts with other programs that use high mem-

ory (such as Microsoft Windows), specify /USEHMA=NO
to disallow NCACHE-F to use this memory. See also
/EXT=*extmem*.

+**W** Enables write-through caching for the specified drive
(the default), causing written blocks to be copied to cache
before they are written to disk. Copying written blocks to
cache uses more CPU cycles, but saves time if the block is
read again.

−**W** Disables write-through caching for the specified drive.
If intelligent writes are enabled (+I), NCACHE-F ignores
this parameter because all writes must be copied to cache.

Notes:

■ Do not attempt to run NCACHE-F and any other disk
drive caching program (such as SMARTDRV.SYS) at the
same time.

■ For maximum compatibility with your system, you
should activate NCACHE-F by including it in your
CONFIG.SYS file. You must start any high memory driv-
ers (such as HIMEM.SYS) before installing NCACHE-F.
You must also include a BUFFERS= command in
CONFIG.SYS with a buffer number of at least 3. A
buffer number larger than 10 is probably not optimal.

■ NCACHE-F allocates a fixed amount of memory for
cache buffers. Unlike the SMARTDRV.SYS cache program, NCACHE-F cannot interact with Microsoft Windows to dynamically expand and shrink extended or
expanded memory usage. NCACHE-F can cache floppy
drives, however, and provides intelligent writes and smart
reads that are not available with SMARTDRV.SYS. If
you run Microsoft Windows regularly, experiment with
both caching programs to see which provides you with op-
timum performance.

■ Figure 3 on the next page shows an NCACHE-F status
screen. Below the screen is the command line used to start
NCACHE-F. Cache Hit Ratio indicates the efficiency of
the NCACHE-F parameters you have selected.

```
┌──────────────────────── Norton Cache ═══════════════════════════┐
│┌═══ DOS Memory ═══┐┌═══ Extended Memory ══┐┌═══ Expanded Memory ═══┐│
││NCACHE-F:      9 K││Cache:        1024 K  ││                       ││
││Cache Manag:  41 K││                      ││                       ││
││Available:   532 K││Available:    1024 K  ││Available:        0 K  ││
│└──────────────────┘└──────────────────────┘└───────────────────────┘│
│ Cache Allocated:    243.0K of 1024.0K   [23.7%]. Now Using: 238.5K   [23.3%] │
│┌════════════════════════ Cache Options ════════════════════════════┐│
││DOS=0K    EXT=1024K    EXP=0K        BLOCK=1K    DELAY=5.0    QUICK=ON││
│└────────────────────────────────────────────────────────────────────┘│
│┌════ Drive Options ════┐          ┌═══ Drive Statistics ═══┐│
││      A  C  I  W  S  R  G          Cache Hit Ratio    %Hits││
││Drive A:  -  +  +  +  +  D8 128         0/0         [00.0%]││
││Drive B:  -  +  +  +  +  D8 128         0/0         [00.0%]││
││Drive C:  +  +  +  +  +  D4 128       166/632       [26.2%]││
││Drive D:  +  +  +  +  +  D8 128         4/24        [16.6%]││
│                                                           │
│C:\>NCACHE-F /B=1K /DE=5 /EXT=1024 /QU=ON A: -A B: -A C: +I R=D4 +S │
│                                                           │
└────────────────────────────────────────────────────────────────────┘
```

Figure 3. *NCACHE-F status screen.*

See also: NCACHE-S.

NCACHE-S
(Slow Norton Disk Cache)

Description:
Speeds up data access by using the computer's memory to
store active blocks and satisfying program reads for those
blocks from memory (which is very fast) rather than disk
(which is very slow). NCACHE-F is usually faster than
NCACHE-S (see the description of NCACHE-F), but
NCACHE-F requires significantly more memory than
NCACHE-S.

Syntax:

5.0   In CONFIG.SYS:

> DEVICE=[*drive:*][*path*]NCACHE-S.EXE [/<u>B</u>LOCK=*blksz*]
> [/<u>DO</u>S=[-]*dosmem*] [/EXT=[-]*extmem*]
> [/EXP=[-]*expmem*] [/<u>USEHI</u>DOS={YES | NO}]
> [/<u>USEHM</u>A={YES | NO}] [[*drive:*] [{+|-}A] [{+|-}C]
> [G=*grpsz*] [{+|-}W]]...

In AUTOEXEC.BAT:

> NCACHE-S [/<u>B</u>LOCK=*blksz*] [/<u>DO</u>S=[-]*dosmem*]
> [/EXT=[-]*extmem*] [/EXP=[-]*expmem*]
> [/<u>USEHI</u>DOS={YES | NO}] [/<u>USEHM</u>A={YES | NO}]
> [[*drive:*] [{+|-}A] [{+|-}C] [G=*grpsz*] [{+|-}W]]...

From the command line:

> NCACHE-F [/<u>B</u>LOCK=*blksz*] [/<u>DO</u>S=[-]*dosmem*]
> [/EXT=[-]*extmem*] [/EXP=[-]*expmem*] [/<u>R</u>ESET]
> [/<u>STA</u>TUS] [/<u>U</u>NINSTALL] [/<u>USEHI</u>DOS={YES | NO}]
> [/<u>USEHM</u>A={YES | NO}] [[*drive:*] [{+|-}A] [{+|-}C] [F]
> [G=*grpsz*] [{+|-}W]]...

Parameters:

drive: The single-letter designator for the drive that contains the NCACHE-S program or the drive you want to affect with switch settings. Follow the letter with a colon. The current drive is the default for the NCACHE-S program location, and all drives is the default for switch settings.

path   The fully qualified name of the directory that contains the NCACHE-S program. The default is the root path for the drive specified.

+A   Activates caching for the specified drive, which is the default.

−A   Deactivates caching for the specified drive if NCACHE-S is already active. Does not activate caching for the specified drive when starting NCACHE-S for the first time.

/BLOCK=*blksz*   Size of the data blocks in memory. You can include this parameter only the first time you invoke

NCACHE-S. Valid values for *blksz* are 512, 1K, 2K, 4K, and 8K. Use a smaller *blksz* if most of your files are small or fragmented.

+C Allow new data being read to be placed in memory cache for the specified drive, which is the default.

−C Do not place any new data being read into memory cache for the specified drive.

/DOS=*dosmem* Indicates the amount of MS-DOS memory (below 640 KB), in KB, that you want NCACHE-S to use for cache buffers. You can include this parameter only the first time you invoke NCACHE-S. If your machine has extended or expanded memory that NCACHE-S can use, NCACHE-S allocates no MS-DOS memory for cache buffers. If no extended or expanded memory is available, the default is 128 KB.

/DOS=*-dosmem* Indicates the amount of MS-DOS memory (below 640 KB) that you want NCACHE-S to leave for other programs. You can include this parameter only the first time you invoke NCACHE-S. If your machine has available extended or expanded memory, the default is to leave as much MS-DOS memory as possible.

/EXT=*extmem* Indicates the amount of extended memory, in KB, that you want to allow NCACHE-S to use. You can include this parameter only the first time you invoke NCACHE-S. The default is to use all available extended memory. If you run applications that use extended memory (such as Microsoft Windows), you should limit the amount of extended memory NCACHE-S consumes so that some is left for these applications. NCACHE-S ignores this parameter if /USEHMA=NO.

/EXT=*-extmem* Indicates the amount of extended memory, in KB, that you want NCACHE-S to leave for other applications. You can include this parameter only the first time you invoke NCACHE-S. The default is to leave no extended memory unallocated.

/EXP=*expmem* Indicates the amount of expanded memory, in KB, that you want to allow NCACHE-S to use. You can include this parameter only the first time you invoke NCACHE-S. The default is to use all available expanded memory. If you run applications that use expanded memory (such as Microsoft Windows), you should limit the amount of expanded memory NCACHE-S consumes so that some is left for these applications.

/EXP=-*expmem* Indicates the amount of expanded memory, in KB, that you want NCACHE-S to leave for other applications. You can include this parameter only the first time you invoke NCACHE-S. The default is to leave no expanded memory unallocated.

/F Clears the cache buffers.

G=*grpsz* Specifies the group sector size. Valid values are 1 through 128, and the default value is 128. A small number limits the number of sectors that can be placed into memory in a single read. A smaller number can improve performance for small random reads.

/RESET Resets cache statistics.

/STATUS Displays the status screen. If you have not installed NCACHE-S and specify no option other than /STATUS, NCACHE-S installs itself using default parameters.

/UNINSTALL Clears all cache buffers and removes NCACHE-S from memory. You cannot uninstall NCACHE-S if you loaded it as a device driver in CONFIG.SYS. Also, NCACHE-S must be the last terminate-and-stay-resident (TSR) program loaded into memory to be able to uninstall it. You can use the –A parameter to disable NCACHE-S without uninstalling it.

/USEHIDOS={YES | NO} YES allows NCACHE-S to use high MS-DOS memory (above 640 KB) if it is available. You can include this parameter only the first time you invoke NCACHE-S. If either extended or expanded memory is available, the default is NO.

/USEHMA={YES | NO} YES (the default) allows
NCACHE-S to use extended memory. You can include this
parameter only the first time you invoke NCACHE-S. If you
encounter conflicts with other programs that use high memory (such as Microsoft Windows), specify /USEHMA=NO
to disallow NCACHE-S to use this memory. See also
/EXT=*extmem*.

+W Enables write-through caching for the specified drive
(the default), causing written blocks to be copied to cache
before they are written to disk. Copying written blocks to
cache uses more CPU cycles but saves time if the block is
read again.

−W Disables write-through caching for the specified drive.

Notes:

■ Do not attempt to run NCACHE-S and any other disk
   drive caching program (such as SMARTDRV.SYS) at the
   same time.

■ For maximum compatibility with your system, you
   should activate NCACHE-S by including it in your
   CONFIG.SYS file. You must start any high memory driv-
   ers (such as HIMEM.SYS) before installing NCACHE-S.
   You must also include a BUFFERS= command in
   CONFIG.SYS with a buffer number of at least 3. A
   buffer number larger than 10 is probably not optimal.

■ NCACHE-S allocates a fixed amount of memory for
   cache buffers. Unlike the SMARTDRV.SYS cache program, NCACHE-S cannot interact with Microsoft Windows to dynamically expand and shrink extended or
   expanded memory usage. NCACHE-S can cache floppy
   drives, however, which SMARTDRV.SYS cannot. If you
   run Microsoft Windows regularly, experiment with both
   caching programs to see which provides you with opti-
   mum performance.

See also: NCACHE-F.

NCC (Norton Control Center)

Description:

Controls system hardware settings such as screen colors, display size, cursor size, serial port configurations, and clock settings.

Syntax:

4.5 NCC [*drive:*][*path*][*filename*] [/D0 | /D1] [/BW] [/NOSNOW]

NCC [[*drive:*][*path*][*filename*] [[/COM*n*] [/<u>CUR</u>SOR] [/<u>DIS</u>PLAY] [/<u>DOS</u>COLOR] [/<u>KEY</u>RATE] [/<u>PAL</u>ETTE]] | /<u>SET</u>ALL]

NCC [/BW80 | /CO80 | /25 | /35 | /40 | /43 | /50] [/<u>FAS</u>TKEY]

5.0 NCC [*drive:*][*path*][*filename*]

NCC [[*drive:*][*path*]*filename* [[/<u>CUR</u>SOR] [/<u>DOS</u>COLOR]] | /SET]

NCC [/BW80] | /CO80 | /25 | /35 | /40 | /43 | /50] [/<u>FAS</u>TKEY]

NCC [/C:*comment*] [/L] [/N] [/<u>STA</u>RT:*n*] [/<u>STO</u>P:*n*]

Parameters:

drive: The single-letter designator for the drive that contains the file in which you previously saved control settings by using NCC. Follow the letter with a colon. The current drive is the default.

path The fully qualified name of the directory that contains the file in which you previously saved control settings by using NCC and selecting the Save option from the File menu. The current directory for the designated drive is the default.

filename The name of the file in which you previously saved control settings by using NCC. See Notes for information about how to use the NCC menu system.

/BW Specifies a black-and-white display.

/BW80 Sets the display mode to black-and-white, 80 columns by 25 rows.

/C:*comment* Specifies the text string you want NCC to display either with the date and time or with the elapsed time value. (In early copies of version 5.0, NCC does not display the text on the line that contains the elapsed time value if you include the /N switch.) You must enclose any text string in quotation marks if it includes one or more blank spaces. If the text string contains a single quotation mark character, enclose the text in double quotation marks. If the text string contains a double quotation mark character, enclose the text in single quotation marks.

/COM*n* Sets only the serial port *n* settings saved in *filename*.

/CO80 Quick-sets the display mode to color, 80 columns by 25 rows.

/CURSOR Sets only the cursor settings saved in *filename*.

/DISPLAY Sets only the display mode saved in *filename*.

/DOSCOLOR Sets the foreground, background, and (for VGA and CGA monitors) border colors, based on values saved in *filename*.

/D0 Requests the standard screen driver (the default) for a fully IBM-compatible computer system.

/D1 Requests the screen driver for a BIOS-compatible computer system.

/FASTKEY Quick-sets the keyboard repeat rate to 30 characters per second with a ¼-second delay.

/KEYRATE Sets only the keyboard speed settings saved in *filename*.

/L Displays the time and date (created with /START) on
the left side of the screen. If you do not include this
switch, NCC displays the time and date on the right side
of the screen.

/N Prevents NCC from displaying the current time and date
and shows only the elapsed time interval.

/NOSNOW Prevents screen flicker if your system has an
older CGA card.

/PALETTE Sets only the color palette settings saved
in *filename*.

/SET Sets all control settings saved in *filename*
(version 5.0).

/SETALL Sets all control settings saved in *filename*.

/START:*n* Resets the specified stopwatch (1 through 4) and
displays the time and date.

/STOP:*n* Displays the time and date and the time that has
elapsed since the last START for the specified stopwatch
(1 through 4). This keyword does not stop the stopwatch.

/25 Quick-sets the display mode to color, 80 columns by 25
rows. (This switch has the same effect as the /CO80 switch.)

/35 Quick-sets the display to color in the EGA display
mode, 80 columns by 35 rows.

/40 Quick-sets the display to color in the VGA display
mode, 80 columns by 40 rows.

/43 Quick-sets the display to color in the EGA display
mode, 80 columns by 43 rows.

/50 Quick-sets the display to color in the VGA mode, 80 columns by 50 rows.

Notes:

■ If you do not supply either set options (in the second syntax line) or a quick-setting (in the third syntax line), or a

stopwatch setting (in the fourth syntax line in version
5.0), NCC displays a full-screen menu you can use to define control settings.

■ When you provide the menu system with a *filename*,
NCC loads the settings from the file and prompts you to
save changes before you leave the menu system.

■ Figure 4 shows the initial menu in version 5.0. Use the
Up and Down direction keys to position the highlight on
one of the ten options. In version 4.5, options to change
Mouse Speed and Country Info are not available. As you
move the highlight, the box on the right side of the menu
changes to match the option. To modify specific options,
begin by pressing Enter, Tab, or the Right direction key
to move the cursor to the box on the right.

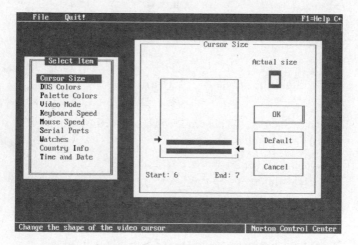

Figure 4. *Norton Control Center initial menu — version 5.0.*

■ After you select an option you want to modify, use the direction keys to move between the various attributes and
to display optional values for the attributes. For example,
on the Cursor Size screen, shown in Figure 4, the Left
and Right direction keys change the option selection between the top (start) and the bottom (end) of the cursor.
The Up and Down direction keys change the position selection for the top and bottom of the cursor. If you have a

mouse, you can also use it to select options from the
menus in version 5.0. In the keyboard speed panel shown
in Figure 5, the Left and Right direction keys change the
cursor speed, and the Up and Down direction keys move
you between the speed and delay options. In version 4.5,
press the Asterisk key (*) to reset values in an option
panel to the default. In version 5.0, select the Default
button to reset to default values. In all panels except the
Watches panel, press Enter to accept the changes you
made. Press Escape to leave the selected panel. If you
have a mouse, you can also use it to move within panels
and select buttons in version 5.0.

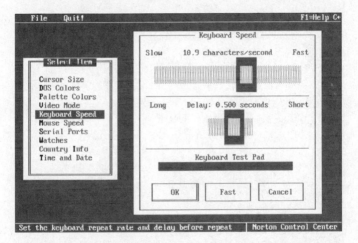

Figure 5. *Norton Control Center keyboard speed menu.*

■ Within the menu system, press F1 to display a Help
panel, and press F2 to save the current settings. In version
4.5, press F10 to leave the menu system. In version 5.0,
press F10 to activate the menu bars at the top of the
screen, and choose Quit! or press Escape to exit.

■ Because a stopwatch runs until you reset it with the
START keyword, you can use successive STOP keywords to measure the elapsed time interval since the
previous START.

■ If START follows STOP on a command line, NCC displays the time that has elapsed and resets and restarts the stopwatch.

See also: BE SA, SI, SYSINFO, TM.

NCD
(Norton Change Directory)

Description:

Creates or removes directories and lets you change to any directory quickly by entering only part of the last qualifier of the directory path. This command can also provide a full-screen menu system that displays the directory tree and lets you maintain or change directories within the tree.

NCD maintains a file named TREEINFO.NCD in the root directory of the drive; TREEINFO.NCD contains quick lookup tables for all directories. This file is created the first time you run NCD on a drive and is updated whenever you run NCD MD or NCD RD or if you use the /R switch with NCD *dirspec*.

Syntax:

4.0   NCD [*drive:*] [/D0 I /D1 I /D2] [[[/F*n*] [/B*n*]] I /BW I /TV]

4.5   NCD [*drive:*] [/D0 I /D1] [/BW] [/NOSNOW]

4.0, 4.5   NCD [*drive:*]*dirspec* [/N] [/R]

NCD MD *dirname*

NCD RD *dirname*

5.0   NCD [*drive:*][*dirspec*] [/N] [/R] [/V:*vlabel*]

NCD MD *dirname*

NCD RD *dirname*

Parameters:

drive: The single letter designator for the drive you want to process. Follow the letter with a colon. The current drive is the default.

dirspec The partial or complete last qualifier of the directory you want to establish as the current directory. You cannot include the parent path names in *dirspec*. NCD compares *dirspec* to the leading characters of the last qualifier for each directory name in the tree, and it establishes as the current directory the next directory whose last qualifier matches *dirspec*. To establish the next matching directory as the current directory, enter NCD using the same *dirspec*. If the last qualifiers for all directories on a disk are unique, NCD requires fewer keystrokes than the MS-DOS CD command does to establish a directory within a complex tree as the current directory.

MD *dirname* Works identically to the MS-DOS MD command, but also updates the TREEINFO.NCD file.

RD *dirname* Works identically to the MS-DOS RD command, but also updates the TREEINFO.NCD file.

/B*n* The background color for the menu system in version 4.0 if you do not specify either *dirspec* or the MD or RD subcommand. Use an integer from 0 through 15 to specify the color. If you attempt to specify identical foreground and background colors, NCD adds 1 to the foreground color number before beginning execution. Avoid using the high-intensity shade of a color for the foreground with the normal-intensity shade of the same color for the background (for example, /F12 bright red and /B4 red). The default is /B1 (blue). See Appendix D.

/BW In versions 4.0 and 4.5, specifies a black-and-white display.

/D0 In versions 4.0 and 4.5, requests the standard screen driver (the default) for a fully IBM-compatible computer system.

/D1 In versions 4.0 and 4.5, requests the screen driver for a BIOS-compatible computer system.

/D2 In versions 4.0 and 4.5, requests the ANSI.SYS driver for a non-IBM-compatible computer system.

/Fn In version 4.0, specifies the foreground color for the menu system if you do not specify either *dirspec* or the MD or RD subcommand. Use an integer from 0 through 15 to specify the color. The default is /F15 (bright white). See Appendix D.

/N Prevents NCD from writing a TREEINFO.NCD file. Include this switch when you run NCD on a write-protected floppy disk.

/NOSNOW In version 4.5, prevents screen flicker if your system has an older CGA card.

/R Rescans the directories and updates TREEINFO.NCD. Include this switch if you used the MS-DOS MD or RD command instead of NCD to change the directory tree structure.

/TV In version 4.0, indicates that NCD is running under either TopView or Microsoft Windows.

/V:*vlabel* In version 5.0, specifies the new label you want to place on the disk. The label can be up to 10 characters long and cannot include any spaces.

Notes:

■ Figure 6 shows the primary display within the full-screen menu system of NCD in version 5.0; the menu system is also available in versions 4.0 and 4.5. In versions 4.0 and later, use the direction keys to move the highlight from one directory to another. Press PgUp and PgDn to move the highlight a page at a time. Press Home to move to the top of the tree and press End to move to the bottom of the tree.

```
┌─────────────────────────────────────────────────────────────────┐
│   Disk    Directory    View    Quit?                    F1=Help   │
│ ╲ ┬─TEST                                                         ↑│
│   └─TOYS──────┬─ANIMALS───────┬─BEARS                            ║│
│               │               ├─LIONS                            ║│
│               │               └─TIGERS                           ║│
│               ├─BUILD─────────┬─BLOCKS                           ║│
│               │               ├─BRICKS                           ║│
│               │               └─LOGS                             ║│
│               ├─CRAFTS────────┬─DRAW                             ║│
│               │               ├─PAINT                            ║│
│               │               └─SEW                              ║│
│               ├─GAMES─────────┬─BACKGAMN                         ║│
│               │               ├─CHECKERS                         ║│
│               │               ├─█CHESS█                          ║│
│               │               ├─DOMINO                           ║│
│               │               └─MONOPOLY                         ║│
│               └─VEHICLES──────┬─BOATS                            ║│
│                               ├─CARS                             ║│
│                               └─PLANES                           ║│
│                               ▼                                 ↓│
│ ←                                                            →↓  │
│ B:╲TOYS╲GAMES╲CHESS                                              │
│ Speed Search: CHES                        Volume label: DATA0804-9│
│ ^Enter=Next match  Enter=Change  Esc=Quit │ Norton Change Directory│
└─────────────────────────────────────────────────────────────────┘
```

Figure 6. *Norton Change Directory screen — version 5.0.*

■ In versions 4.5 and later, you can search for a particular directory by entering one or more characters of the last qualifier of the directory path: Speed Search stops on the next directory whose last qualifier begins with the characters you entered. Press Ctrl-Enter to continue the search for the next matching directory.

■ When the highlight is on the directory you want, press Enter to make that directory current and to leave NCD.

■ In versions 4.5 and later, press F2 to rescan the directories on the disk and to rebuild TREEINFO.NCD. (This is the same as using the /R switch.) Press F3 to call up the submenu to select a new drive. Use the direction keys to move the highlight to the drive you want and then press Enter, or press Escape to leave drive selection.

■ Move the highlight to the name of a directory you want to modify. Then press F6 in versions 4.5 and later or the letter R in version 4.0 to rename the directory. (You can rename a directory only if you are using MS-DOS version 3.0 or later.) Press F7 in versions 4.5 and later or the letter M in version 4.0 to create a new subdirectory under this directory. Press F8 in versions 4.5 and later or the letter D in version 4.0 to delete the directory. You can delete a directory only if it is empty. There is no prompt or request for confirmation.

■ If you have either an EGA or a VGA monitor, you can change the number of lines on the display by pressing F9. Use the direction keys to select the number of lines you want from the submenu.

■ In version 5.0, use F10 to activate the menus at the top of the screen.

■ Version 5.0 also provides mouse support. Move the mouse pointer to the directory or menu bar and click to select it.

■ In the NCD menu system in version 5.0, press Alt-V to assign a new volume label. Press Alt-P to print the directory tree.

■ You can leave the NCD menu system at any time by pressing Escape. In versions 4.5 and earlier, you can also use F10 to quit.

Example:

To reset the current directory to the next directory whose name begins with the letters GA, enter

```
NCD ga
```

See also: LD, VL.

NDD (Norton Disk Doctor)

Description:

Analyzes one or more disks and corrects the problems it finds. If you run NDD without either the /COMPLETE or the /QUICK switch, NDD presents you with a full-screen menu you can use to set options and perform a diagnostic scan. In version 4.5, the NDD Common Solutions menu also provides options that solve certain common problems; in version 5.0, these options are provided in DiskTools. See Notes for details about the menu system.

Syntax:

4.5   (Advanced Edition Only)

> NDD [*drive*:...] [/COMPLETE I /QUICK] [/D0 I /D1] [/BW]
>   [/NOSNOW] [/R:*filename* I /RA:*filename*] [/TYPE*n*]

5.0   NDD [*drive*:...] [/COMPLETE I /QUICK] [/R:*filename* I
>   /RA:*filename*] [/X:*drvltrs*]

Parameters:

drive: The single-letter designator for the drive you want to process. Follow the letter with a colon. To process more than one drive, provide multiple drive designators, separating each of these with a space. The current drive is the default.

/BW In version 4.5, specifies a black-and-white display.

/D0 In version 4.5, requests the standard screen driver (the default) for a fully IBM-compatible computer system.

/D1 In version 4.5, requests the screen driver for a BIOS-compatible computer system.

/COMPLETE Performs a complete analysis of the specified disk, including all tests performed by /QUICK. In addition, the analysis /COMPLETE performs includes reading all data sectors and attempting to move data in allocated unusable sectors to new locations.

/NOSNOW In version 4.5, prevents screen flicker if your system has an older CGA card.

/QUICK Performs a quick diagnosis of the boot record, the file allocation tables, and the directory tree structure. /QUICK does not analyze data sectors.

/R:*filename* Produces a report about the results of running NDD and stores the report in the named file. The *filename* can include a drive and a path. If the file does not already exist, NDD creates it in the current directory on the default disk. If the file already exists, NDD overwrites it without first prompting you for confirmation.

/RA:*filename* Produces a report about the results of running NDD and appends it to the named file. The *filename* can include a drive and a path. If the file does not already exist, NDD does not produce the report.

/TYPE*n* In version 4.5, overrides the drive type for the primary hard drive. You might need to enter this parameter if your system setup values are incorrect for your primary hard drive. To run NDD on a portable system that uses RAM as a primary hard drive, enter /TYPE1 and instruct NDD to proceed when you see the message, "NDD doesn't recognize the Drive Type on Hard Disk 1." You can also use NDD on a portable system to analyze either floppy disks or hard drives, but you cannot use NDD to analyze virtual (RAM) disks.

/X:*drvltrs* Excludes the specified drives from testing. Some manufacturers' versions of MS-DOS allocate drive letters to disk drives that do not exist; use this switch to inform NDD that these drive letters are invalid.

Notes:

■ If you do not specifically request either a complete or a quick analysis with the /COMPLETE or the /QUICK switch, NDD presents you with a full-screen menu. In version 4.5, you can choose Diagnose Disk to execute disk diagnostics, Common Solutions to perform selected recovery options, or Exit Disk Doctor to leave the utility. In version 5.0, you can choose Diagnose Disk to execute disk diagnostics, Undo Changes to reverse changes made by Disk Doctor, Options to set diagnostic options, or Quit Disk Doctor to leave the utility.

■ If you select the Diagnose Disk option from the main menu, NDD first asks you to select which of the drives you want to diagnose from among those it detected on the system. For each drive you select, NDD checks the boot record, the file allocation tables, and the directory structure. (This diagnosis is identical to the /QUICK switch option.) When the quick diagnosis is completed, NDD asks you whether you would also like to test all data sectors on the selected drives. (This diagnosis is identical to the /COMPLETE switch option.) Graphic displays show the progress of each test as it is executed. After all tests are complete, you can produce a report of the results, which NDD displays; you can also direct the report to a file or your system printer.

■ In version 4.5, Common Solutions provides three specific recovery options. The first option, Make a Disk Bootable, lets you rebuild a disk system area to make it bootable; this rebuild includes copying the MS-DOS COMMAND.COM, IO.SYS, and MSDOS.SYS files from the current system disk. Using the second option, Recover from DOS's RECOVER, you can rebuild the subdirectories and the root directory entries on a disk when you have used the MS-DOS RECOVER command to attempt to recover the disk. The third option, Revive a Defective Diskette, lets you recover the data on a defective floppy disk by rewriting the format information. (Unlike an MS-DOS FORMAT command, this option reformats without destroying the original data.) All of these options are incorporated in DISKTOOL in version 5.0.

See also: DISKTOOL, FR, NU, SFORMAT, UNERASE, UNFORMAT.

NI (Norton Integrator)

Description:
Provides a full-screen menu system that lets you run any Norton utility by selecting it from the menu. You can enter parameters and option switches in a command edit window before you run the selected utility. NI provides help for each utility in the box on the right.

Syntax:

4.0   NI [/D0 | /D1 | /D2] [[[/F*n*] [/B*n*]] | /BW | /TV]

4.5   NI [/D0 | /D1] [/BW] [/NOSNOW]

5.0   *See* NORTON

Parameters:

/B*n* In version 4.0, specifies the background color for the menu system. Use an integer from 0 through 15 to specify the color. If you attempt to specify identical foreground and background colors, NI adds one to the foreground color number before beginning execution. Avoid using the high-intensity shade of a color for the foreground with the normal-intensity shade of the same color for the background (for example, /F12 bright red and /B4 red). The default is /B1 (blue). See Appendix D.

/BW Specifies a black-and-white display in versions 4.0 and 4.5.

/D0 Requests the standard screen driver (the default) for a fully IBM-compatible computer system.

/D1 Requests the screen driver for a BIOS-compatible computer system.

/D2 In version 4.0, requests the ANSI.SYS driver for a non-IBM-compatible computer system.

/F*n* In version 4.0, specifies the foreground color for the menu system. Use an integer from 0 through 15 to specify the color. The default is /F15 (bright white). See Appendix D.

/NOSNOW Prevents screen flicker if your system has an older CGA card.

/TV In version 4.0, indicates that NI is running under either TopView or Microsoft Windows.

Notes:

- Figure 7 shows the primary screen in the Advanced Edition of version 4.5 of the Norton Integrator. Use the Up and Down direction keys to change the command

selection on the left side of the panel. The right side of the
panel shows the syntax and a brief description of each
command when you select it. You can also use the PgUp
and PgDn keys to page through all available command selections rapidly. Press the Tab key to enter Speed Search
mode; this allows you to type either all or part of a command name to move the highlight to the matching command name that is closest in the list. When the highlight
is on the command you want, press the Tab key again to
leave Speed Search mode. Type additional parameters or
switches to complete the selected command. You can use
WordStar-compatible edit keys within the command edit
window. When you have completed the command, press
Enter to run it.

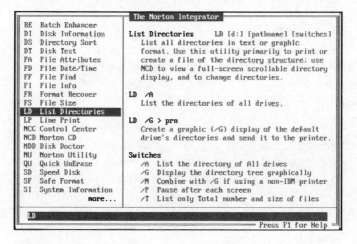

Figure 7. *Norton Integrator screen — version 4.5.*

- NI is incorporated in the NORTON command in
  version 5.0.

- When a command you have initiated from within NI completes execution, the NI menu reappears. The Norton Integrator keeps a history of the NI commands you have run
  in this session. Press Ctrl-E to move backward in the

history list, and press Ctrl-X to move forward. You can
modify and run any previously executed command again
by pressing Enter when it is displayed.

■ If you start NI with one of the display switches (such as
/BW) and if you intend to run one of the other full-screen
commands using the attribute indicated by the switch,
you must reenter the switch on the command line. In version 4.5, the full-screen commands are DS, FR, NCC,
NCD, NDD, NU, SD, and SF. In version 4.0, they are DS,
NCD, NU, and SD.

NORTON

Description:

Provides a full-screen menu system that lets you run any
Norton utility by selecting it. Before you run the selected
utility, you can enter parameters and option switches in a
command line window at the bottom of the screen. You
can also configure NORTON to run any program or batch
file that you can invoke from an MS-DOS command line.
NORTON includes a description of each command in the
Description box on the right, as well as complete help information about each command when you press F1. In addition,
NORTON provides extensive advice about many common
problems.

Syntax:

5.0   NORTON

Notes:

■ Figure 8 shows the main menu of the version 5.0
NORTON utility. Use the Up and Down direction keys
or the mouse to scroll through or select from the commands in the Commands box on the left of the screen.
As you select each command or command category,
NORTON displays help information in the Description
box on the right. For each command, NORTON displays

the basic command syntax in the command line window
at the bottom of the screen (see Figure 9). You can enter
parameters such as filenames and switches before pressing Enter or double-clicking the mouse to execute the
command. Initially, NORTON displays the commands
within categories (RECOVERY, SPEED, SECURITY,
TOOLS). You can choose to display the commands in alphabetic order without the categories by selecting Sort by
Name from the Configure menu.

Figure 8. *NORTON main menu — version 5.0.*

Figure 9. *NORTON main menu and command line window.*

■ You can customize the NORTON menu system to add
your own categories, commands, and help text. Press F10
or select Configure from the menu bar to open the Configuration options menu. Select Add menu item (see
Figure 10) to create a new command or topic. Select Command; in the dialog box, give the command a descriptive
title, enter the MS-DOS command to be executed, and select a Topic for the command to be grouped with. Select
the Description button to enter help text about the command (see Figure 11). After you complete the Add Menu
Item dialog box, the new command is selected in the
NORTON menu. Note that if the command you add must
run in a different directory from the one in which you run
NORTON, you should use a batch file with a CD command to change directories before running the command.
Figure 12 shows a sample custom menu group for communications programs.

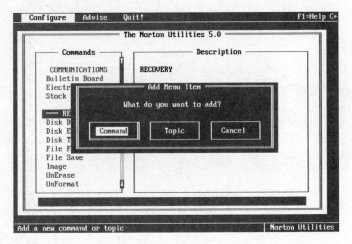

Figure 10. *Add menu item options.*

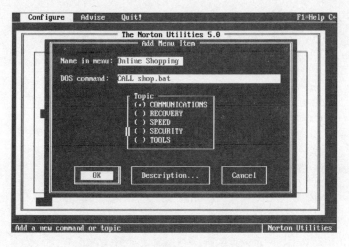

Figure 11.   *Add menu item command dialog box.*

Figure 12.   *Sample Norton custom menu group.*

■ The Configure menu provides video and mouse options,
which include screen colors, screen options, graphics options, and mouse options. The Advise menu offers solutions to many common disk problems.

NU (Norton Utilities Main Program)

Description:

Runs a full-screen menu utility that displays information about a disk, lets you scan and edit information on a disk, and recovers deleted files and lost data.

Syntax:

3.0   NU [*drive*:] [/D0 | /D1 | /D2] [/<u>NO</u>COLOR | /TV]

3.1   NU [*drive*:] [/D0 | /D1 | /D2] [[[/F*n*] [/B*n*]] | /NOC | /TV] [/EBCDIC] [/EUR] [/P]

4.0   NU [*drive*:][*path*][*filename*] [/D0 | /D1 | /D2] [[[/F*n*] [/B*n*]] | /BW | /TV] [/EBCDIC] [/EXT] [/M] [/P] [/x:*drvltrs*]

4.5   NU [*drive*:][*path*][*filename*] [/D0 | /D1] [/BW] [/EBCDIC] [/M] [/NOSNOW] [/P] [/WS] [/X:*drvltrs*]

5.0   *See* DISKEDIT, DISKTOOL, UNERASE

Parameters:

drive: The single-letter designator for the drive you want to process. Follow the letter with a colon. The current drive is the default.

path The fully qualified name of the directory that NU initially selects for further processing. The current directory is the default.

filename The name of the file you want to display. If the *filename* you supply does not exist, no data is displayed. The default *filename* is *.*.

/B*n* Specifies the background color for the menu system. Use an integer from 0 through 15 to specify the color. Within the menu system, you can add 1 to *n* by pressing F3. In version 3.1, you can specify identical foreground and background colors, but much of the information on the screen will be unreadable. In version 4.0, if you attempt to specify identical foreground and background colors, NU adds 1 to the foreground color number before beginning execution. Avoid using the high-intensity shade of a color for the foreground with the normal-intensity shade of the same color for the background (for example, /F12 bright red and /B4 red). The default is /B1 (blue). See Appendix D.

/BW Specifies a black-and-white display in versions 4.0 and 4.5. Within the menu system, you can use F1 to turn this switch on and off.

/D0 Requests the standard screen driver (the default) for a fully IBM-compatible computer system.

/D1 Requests the screen driver for a BIOS-compatible computer system.

/D2 Requests the ANSI.SYS driver for a non-IBM-compatible computer system.

/EBCDIC Displays characters using the Extended Binary Coded Decimal Interchange Code rather than ASCII. Within the menu system, you can use Alt-F5 to turn this switch on and off.

/EUR In version 3.1, specifies the European character set and displays character codes 128 through 255 without alteration. The default is to remove the high-order bit from all characters to restrict the characters displayed to the codes 0 through 127. Within the menu system, you can use Alt-F6 to turn this switch on and off.

/EXT In version 4.0, specifies the extended character set and displays all characters without modification. If you do not use this switch, NU removes the high-order bit from all characters to restrict the characters displayed to the codes 0 through 127. Within the menu system, you can use Alt-F6 to turn this switch on and off.

/F*n* Specifies the foreground color for the menu system. Use an integer from 0 through 15 to specify the color. In the menu system, you can press F4 to add 1 to the value of *n*. The default is /F15 (bright white). See Appendix D.

/M (Advanced Edition only.) Sets maintenance mode to allow NU to bypass the MS-DOS logical structure. Use this switch if you are working with a badly damaged disk.

/NOC Specifies a black-and-white display in versions 3.0 and 3.1. Within the menu system, you can use F1 to turn this switch on and off.

/NOSNOW Prevents screen flicker if your system has an older CGA card.

/P Suppresses display of nonprintable characters. Within the menu system, you can use Alt-F2 to turn this switch on and off.

/TV Indicates that the utility is running under either TopView or Microsoft Windows.

/WS Sets WordStar character display mode. Removes the high-order bit from all characters to restrict the range of display characters to codes 0 through 127. The default in version 4.5 is to display all character codes without alteration. Within the menu system, you can use Alt-F6 to turn this switch on and off.

/X:*drvltrs* (Advanced Edition only.) Excludes specified drives from processing. Some manufacturers' versions of MS-DOS allocate drive letters to disk drives that do not exist; use this switch to inform NU that these drive letters are invalid.

Notes:

■ In versions 4.0 and 4.5, the main menu of NU provides you with three options: You can choose Explore disk to explore and change data on your disk; UnErase to execute the UnErase file subsystem; or Disk information to display information about any of your disk drives. In versions 3.0 and 3.1, the options on the main menu let you select a drive, file, disk directory, or disk sector, and they let you either explore and change data on your disk or execute the Unerase file submenus. In versions 4.0 and later, selecting a drive, file, disk directory, or disk sector is a subfunction of Explore disk.

■ In all versions, you can use the Explore disk functions to search files, directories, or sectors for specific information, to display information about items you have selected, and to display data that is on your disk in hexadecimal, text, or directory format. When your data is displayed in hexadecimal format, you can modify it and request NU to write it back to disk. If you are using the Advanced Edition of either version 4.0 or version 4.5, you can change your data when it is in directory format display mode, you can edit and change the file allocation table (FAT) and the partition table, and you can scan the disk by absolute cluster address.

Caution: *If you change data in directories, in the FAT, in the partition table, or in the boot record, you can lose data or render your disk unusable.*

■ In all versions, you can use the Unerase file submenus to select the directory you want to search for missing file entries, to pick a found entry for an erased file, to examine the data in the clusters that were occupied by the deleted file, and to restore the filename and the space it occupied. (Note that MS-DOS does not actually erase a deleted file; instead, it changes the first character of the file's name in the directory and marks each FAT entry allocated to that file as available.) You can manually add specific clusters to a deleted file. In versions 4.0 and 4.5, you can also create a new file directory entry if the original file directory entry has been overwritten, and you can easily add, reorder, and delete clusters associated with a particular file.

■ NU functions are incorporated in the DISKEDIT, DISKTOOL, and UNERASE commands in version 5.0.

See also: DI, DISKEDIT, DISKTOOL, FR, NCD, QU, SF, TS, UD, UNERASE.

QU (Quick UnErase)

Description:

Recovers erased files in a selected directory if the file's primary cluster has not been reallocated to another file. You can direct QU either to provide a unique first character for a file or to prompt you for a character. If a file is larger than one cluster, QU makes a "best guess" when reallocating clusters to the erased file.

Syntax:

3.1   QU [*drive:*][*path*] [/A]

4.0, 4.5   QU [*drive:*][*path*][*filename*] [/A]

5.0   *See* UNERASE

Parameters:

drive: The single-letter designator for the drive you want to use. Follow the letter with a colon. The current drive is the default.

path The fully qualified name of the directory you want to search for deleted files. The current directory for the designated drive is the default.

filename The name of the file you want to unerase. For example, enter QU *.BAT if you want to unerase all files with the extension BAT. If you supply the first character for the filename pattern, QU unerases all files whose names match the pattern and prompts you for acknowledgment or for a first character only if erased filenames were identical except for the first character.

/A Requests QU to generate erased filenames. In versions 4.0 and 4.5, if you do not use this switch and you do not specify the first character of the file in *filename*, QU prompts you to confirm each file to be unerased and asks you to

provide the first character for each candidate file. After you
run QU with this switch, use the MS-DOS RENAME command to correct the names of the restored files.

Note:

■ Because QU makes a "best guess" about the clusters that
originally belonged to a multiple-cluster file, the utility
might not always unerase the file correctly. If a file does
not contain the data you expected after you restore it with
QU, delete the file again and use the NU unerase file func-
tion to search for the clusters that should be assigned to
the file.

■ QU is incorporated in the UNERASE command in
version 5.0.

Example:

To restore all erased files in the GAMES directory in
drive B, enter

```
QU b:\games /A
```

See also: DI, FR, NCD, NU, SF, TS, UD, UNERASE.

SA (Screen Attributes)

Description:
Sets screen attributes.

Syntax:
3.0, 3.1, 4.0 SA <u>NORMAL</u> [/N]

SA [<u>BLINKING</u>] [<u>BRIGHT</u> | <u>BOLD</u>] <u>REVERSE</u>
[/N]

SA [<u>BLINKING</u>] [<u>BRIGHT</u> | <u>BOLD</u>]
<u>UNDERLINE</u> [/N]

SA [[<u>BLINKING</u>] [<u>BRIGHT</u> | <u>BOLD</u>]
[*fore-color*] [[ON] *back-color*]] [/N]

4.5, 5.0   *See* BE SA

Parameters:

BLINKING   Causes the message to repeatedly blink on and off. On some monitors, this keyword works only if you specify *back-color*.

BRIGHT | BOLD   Displays the foreground in high intensity.

NORMAL   Erases the screen and resets the screen to the standard colors for your display adapter.

REVERSE   Erases the screen and sets the screen display to reverse video.

UNDERLINE   Sets the screen display to underline mode and erases the screen. On some display adapters this keyword resets the default to color characters on a black background.

fore-color   Specifies the foreground color for screen displays such as messages, box lines, and window frame lines. The default foreground color is white.

back-color   Specifies the background color for screen displays. If you do not provide *fore-color*, you must include the ON keyword. The default background color is black.

/N   Does not reset the border color when the display is in either CGA mode or VGA mode. This switch does not affect the EGA display mode.

Notes:

- You must have already installed the ANSI.SYS driver to use this utility.

- SA is incorporated into the BE (Batch Enhancer) utility in versions 4.5 and later.

See also: BE, NCC, Appendix D.

SFORMAT (Safe Format)

Description:

Formats a disk. This command provides options that let you format a disk without destroying information you can use to recover files later.

Syntax:

4.5   SF [*drive*:] [/A] [/B | /S] [/BW] [/C] [/D] [/D0 | /D1]
        [/NOSNOW] [/Q] [/V:*label*] [/1 | /4 | /8 | *size* |
        [/N:*n* /T:*n*]]

5.0   SFORMAT [*drive*:] [/A] [/B | /S] [/D] [/Q] [/V:*label*]
        [/1 | /4 | /8 | *size* | [/N:*n* /T:*n*]]

Parameters:

drive: The single-letter designator for the drive you want to format. Follow the letter with a colon. If you do not specify a drive on the command line, the Safe Format dialog box prompts you to select a drive. In version 5.0, before you can specify a hard disk for *drive*, you must allow hard disk formatting. Choose Hard disks from the Configure menu when the Safe Format dialog box is displayed.

/A Indicates automatic mode. To use this switch, you must specify the *drive*: parameter. If you include this switch, Safe Format begins formatting without presenting you with a menu that lets you change options. Use this switch to run the command from a batch file. If you use this switch, the version 4.5 switches /BW, /D0, /D1, and /NOSNOW remain functional because Safe Format displays a work-in-progress screen. You cannot use this switch and specify a hard disk for *drive* in version 5.0 if you have not previously allowed hard-disk formatting in the SFORMAT Configure menu.

/B Leaves space for system files but does not copy them.

/BW In version 4.5, specifies a black-and-white display.

/C Performs a Complete Format, which includes reformatting unusable sectors. You can use this switch only when running Safe Format with a floppy drive.

/D Performs a standard MS-DOS format. Note that when you include this switch, data on a floppy drive is erased and cannot be recovered.

/D0 In version 4.5, requests the standard screen driver (default) for a fully IBM-compatible computer system. This switch also sets the /D switch.

/D1 In version 4.5, requests the screen driver for a BIOS-compatible computer system. This switch also sets the /D switch.

/N:*n* Specifies the number of sectors per track. The values that are valid for *n* are 8, 9, 15, and 18. If you use /N:*n*, you must also use the /T:*n* switch.

/NOSNOW In version 4.5, prevents screen flicker if your system has an older CGA card.

/Q Performs a Quick Format, which rewrites only the system area and does not erase any part of the data area.

/S Copies the system files to the disk. This makes the disk bootable.

/T:*n* Specifies the number of tracks for a floppy disk. The values that are valid for *n* are 40 and 80. If you use /T:*n*, you must also use the /N:*n* switch.

/V:*label* Specifies the 1- to 11-character string Safe Format writes as the volume label when the format is complete.

/1 Specifies single-sided floppy disk format.

/4 Formats a 360-KB floppy disk in a 1.2-MB drive.

/8 Formats eight sectors per track.

/*size* Specifies the amount of data you can put on a floppy disk. The sizes that are valid for a 5¼-inch disk include 160, 180, 320, 360, and 1200. The sizes that are valid for a 3½-inch disk are 720 and 1440.

Notes:

■ If you use either the Safe Format mode or the Complete
Format mode, the information the FR (Format Recover)
or UNFORMAT command needs is saved on the disk before Safe Format begins formatting. If the disk you want
to format contains data, Safe Format prompts you to verify that you want to format the disk before proceeding.

■ If you did not use command line switches to set the format options or if you used the switches to set incorrect
options, use the dialog selections to set the options before
you select Begin Format from the dialog box. Figure 13
shows the Safe Format dialog box in version 5.0.

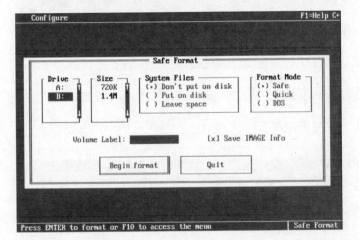

Figure 13.   *Safe Format dialog box — version 5.0.*

■ In version 5.0, you cannot format a hard disk with Safe
Format from the command line or from the dialog box unless you first allow hard disk formatting. Check the box
next to Allow Hard Disk Formatting; the hard disk drive
letters will appear in the list of drives in the dialog box,
and you then can specify a hard disk in the command line.

■ Figure 14 on the next page shows the Format Progress
screen Safe Format displays while a format is in progress.
Safe Format updates this screen as it formats the disk.

```
 Configure                                               F1=Help C←
┌──────────────────────── Formatting B: ─────────────────────────┐
│  ┌─────────────────────────────────────────────────────────┐  │
│  │   Drive: B:              System Mode: No system files     │  │
│  │   Size: 720K             Format Mode: Safe                │  │
│  │   Volume: No Volume Label  IMAGE Info: Saved              │  │
│  │                                                           │  │
│  │  ┌──────────────────────────┐  ┌─────────────────────┐   │  │
│  │  │ Formatting Cylinder 18, Head 1 │  Total Space:  720 K │   │  │
│  │  │                          │   System Space: -   0 K │   │  │
│  │  │ ▓▓▓▓                     │      Bad Space: -   0 K │   │  │
│  │  │        23% Complete      │  ─────────────────────  │   │  │
│  │  └──────────────────────────┘   Usable Space:  720 K │   │  │
│  │                                 └─────────────────────┘   │  │
│  │  ┌──────────────────────────┐                             │  │
│  │  │ Estimated Time: 00:01:05 │     ┌──────────┐            │  │
│  │  │ Elapsed Time: 00:00:15   │     │   Stop   │            │  │
│  │  └──────────────────────────┘     └──────────┘            │  │
│  └─────────────────────────────────────────────────────────┘  │
└────────────────────────────────────────────────────────────────┘
 Press ESC or click the mouse to ABORT              Safe Format
```

Figure 14. *Safe Format Format Progress Screen.*

■ When you install Norton Utilities Version 5.0, one option gives SFORMAT a short name of SF. If you used the short name, use SF instead of SFORMAT.

See also: DP, FR, IMAGE, NU, QU, UD, UNFORMAT.

SPEEDISK (Speed Disk)

Description:

Increases data access speed by moving allocated data fragments so that each directory or file is stored in contiguous space. This command also lets you produce a report about file, directory, or drive fragmentation. In version 4.5, you can specify the priority order for frequently used directories and files. In version 5.0, you can also use Speed Disk to sort directory entries.

Syntax:

4.0   (Advanced Edition only)

   SD [*drive:*] [/A] [/D0 | /D1 | D2] [[[/F*n*] [/B*n*]] | /BW | /TV]

   SD [*drive:*] [*path*] [*filename*] [/REPORT [/P] [/S] [/T]]

4.5   (Advanced Edition only)

   SD [*drive:*] [/A] [/C] [/D] [/P] [/Q] [/U] [/V] [/D0 | /D1]
      [/BW] [/NOSNOW]

   SD [*drive:*][*path*][*filename*] [/REPORT [/P] [/S] [/T]]

5.0   SPEEDISK [*drive:*] [/B] [/C | /D | /Q | /U] [/SD[-] | /SE[-] |
      /SN[-] | /SS[-]] [/V]

Parameters:

drive: The single-letter designator for the drive you want to
process. Follow the letter with a colon. If you do not specify
a drive on the command line, a dialog box prompts you to select a drive.

path The fully qualified name of the directory that Speed
Disk initially selects for processing if you include the
/REPORT switch. The current directory for the designated
drive is the default.

filename The name of the file(s) for which you want to produce a fragmentation report. (See /REPORT.) The default
filename is *.*.

/A Rearranges disk allocation without prompting for
verification. Use this switch if you run Speed Disk from a
batch file.

/B Boots your computer after Speed Disk completes
optimization.

/B*n* Specifies the background color for the screen displays.
Use an integer from 0 through 15 to specify the color. If you
attempt to specify identical foreground and background colors, Speed Disk adds 1 to the foreground color number before beginning execution. Avoid using the high-intensity
shade of a color for the foreground with the normal-intensity

shade of the same color for the background (for example, /F12 bright red and /B4 red). The default is /B1 (blue). See Appendix D.

/BW In version 4.5, specifies a black-and-white display.

/C Requests complete optimization. In version 4.5, establishes Complete Optimization as the default Optimization Method in the Set Options menu. Initiate complete optimization by pressing Enter when the main menu is displayed. In version 5.0, Speed Disk begins complete optimization of the specified drive without pausing for confirmation.

/D Requests optimization of directories only. This option unfragments directories only. In version 4.5, establishes Optimize Directories as the default Optimization Method in the Set Options menu. Initiate directories optimization by pressing Enter when the main menu is displayed. In version 5.0, Speed Disk begins directory optimization of the specified drive without pausing for confirmation. Speed Disk ignores this switch if you specify /C, /Q, or /U.

/D0 Requests the standard screen driver (the default) for a fully IBM-compatible computer system. This switch also sets the /D switch in version 4.5.

/D1 Requests the screen driver for a BIOS-compatible computer system. This switch also sets the /D switch in version 4.5.

/D2 Requests the ANSI.SYS driver for a non-IBM-compatible computer system.

/F*n* Specifies the foreground color for the full-screen displays. Use an integer from 0 through 15 to specify the color. The default is /F15 (bright white). See Appendix D.

/NOSNOW In version 4.5, prevents screen flicker if your system has an older CGA card.

/P If you do not include the /REPORT switch, suppresses display of nonprintable characters on the screen; when you use this display mode, however, you cannot distinguish between used and unused blocks. If you include the /REPORT switch, using /P means that Speed Disk displays the report in pause mode: You initially see one screenful of information, and you must press the Spacebar to see the next screenful.

Press Enter to scroll up one line at a time. Press any key other than Spacebar, Enter, or Escape to leave pause mode. You can also enter pause mode during normal display by pressing any key other than Escape.

/Q Requests quick compress optimization only. This option packs the data at the beginning of the disk but does not unfragment files. In version 4.5, establishes quick compress optimization as the default option in the Optimize Disk menu. Initiate quick optimization by pressing Enter when the menu is displayed. In version 5.0, Speed Disk begins quick compression without pausing for confirmation. Speed Disk ignores this switch if you specify /C or /U.

/REPORT Produces a fragmentation report only. This option produces the report for all files whose names match *filename* in *path*. The default *filename* is *.*. A summary total for the entire drive is also displayed. You can direct the report to either a printer or a file by using the MS-DOS output redirection character (>) followed by a printer name or a filename at the end of the command.

/S Processes all files whose names match *filename* in all subdirectories under the current or specified path.

/SD[−] Sorts directory entries by date. Include the minus sign to sort in descending sequence. In early copies of version 5.0, Speed Disk ignores this switch.

/SE[−] Sorts directory entries by file extension. Include the minus sign to sort in descending sequence. In early copies of version 5.0, Speed Disk ignores this switch.

/SN[−] Sorts directory entries by file name. Include the minus sign to sort in descending sequence. In early copies of version 5.0, Speed Disk ignores this switch.

/SS[–] Sorts directory entries by file size. Include the minus sign to sort in descending sequence. In early copies of version 5.0, Speed Disk ignores this switch.

/T Shows the fragmentation totals only when Speed Disk produces a report. A total is displayed for each directory. If Speed Disk is in pause mode (see /P), the utility might pause several times before you see a total.

/TV In version 4.5, indicates that the utility is running under either TopView or Microsoft Windows.

/U Requests file unfragmentation only. The utility attempts to unfragment files as much as possible without moving files that are already contiguous. In version 4.5, establishes File Unfragment as the default Optimization Method in the Set Options menu. Initiate file unfragmentation by pressing Enter when the main menu is displayed. In version 5.0, Speed Disk begins file unfragmentation without pausing for confirmation. Speed Disk ignores this switch if you specify /C.

/V Verifies that data is written to the disk accurately.

Notes:

■ Do not turn off your computer while Speed Disk is reorganizing your disk or your disk might be damaged. Note that Speed Disk might take 30 minutes or more to reorganize a large hard drive. You can safely interrupt the process at any point by pressing Escape; Speed Disk finishes any reorganization in progress before halting.

■ Back up your disk before running Speed Disk. Some copy-protection schemes might be incompatible with the reorganization Speed Disk performs.

■ Before running Speed Disk, be sure to stop any memory-resident programs that might access the disk while the disk is being reorganized.

■ After Speed Disk has finished reorganizing your disk in versions 4.0 and 4.5, the utility asks you whether you want to reboot your computer. Reboot if you are using the Fastopen program in MS-DOS version 3.3 or later

or if you have a RAM disk installed. Include the /B
switch in version 5.0 to cause an automatic reboot of
your computer.

■ When you install Norton Utilities Version 5.0, one
option gives Speed Disk a short name of SD. If you used
the short name, use SD instead of SPEEDISK in the syntax line.

■ Figure 15 shows the initial version 5.0 Speed Disk screen
you see when you specify no compression options
(switches /C, /D, /Q, and /U). Speed Disk analyzes the
drive you specify and recommends a compression action.
To alter the compression options, select the Configure
box with the mouse or by pressing Tab and Enter.

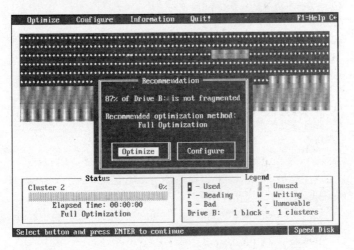

Figure 15. *Norton Speed Disk initial screen — version 5.0.*

■ Figure 16 on the next page shows the version 5.0 Speed
Disk screen after you select Configure from the initial
screen or from the menu at the top of the screen. Activate
the menu with F10. Choose Directory order to define directory priority; for more information, see the Note
below. Choose File sort to specify the order for directory
entries. Speed Disk ignores sorting parameters in early
copies of version 5.0. Choose Files to Place first to reset
file priority; Speed Disk makes files with the extensions

EXE or COM first on the disk. Choose Unmovable files
to name files you do not want Speed Disk to move, such
as copy-protected program files. Under Other options,
you can set the method of read verification and choose to
clear all unused space when done. Select Save options to
disk to create a hidden SD.INI file in the root directory of
the disk.

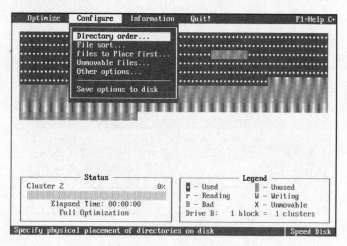

Figure 16. *Norton Speed Disk configuration options menu.*

The Optimize menu on the main menu bar lets you start
optimization, select a different drive, or select the Complete Optimization, File Unfragment, Quick Compress, or
only Optimize Directories options which correspond to
the /C, /U, /D switches.

The Information menu on the main menu bar lets you
view Disk statistics, show the Map legend, Show static
files, Walk map (to select any cluster to see which file is
stored there), and generate a Fragmentation report.

■ When you are using Full optimization or Directory optimization, you can specify the order in which Speed Disk
should arrange directories. Choose Directory order from
the Configure menu; the select Directory Order dialog
box shown in Figure 17 appears. The left side of the box
shows the existing directory tree. Highlight the directory

names in the desired sequence and press Enter to specify
the order in which directories are to be stored on the disk.
Selected directories are shown on the right side of the
box. Press Tab to move to the right side to reorder or delete selected directories or to indicate that you have finished defining directory priority.

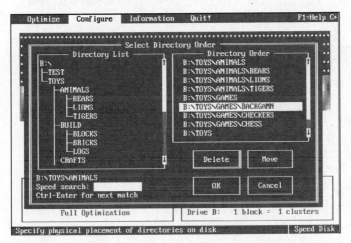

Figure 17. *Norton Speed Disk Directory order menu.*

See also: CALIBRAT, NCACHE-F, NCACHE-S.

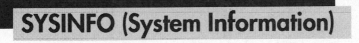

SYSINFO (System Information)

Description:

Tests your computer's configuration and performance. This
command reports the results relative to the configuration and
performance of an IBM PC/XT and, in version 5.0, an IBM
PC/AT and a Compaq 386.

Syntax:

3.0 SI

3.1 SI [/N]

4.0, 4.5   SI [*drive*:] [/A] [/LOG] [/N]

5.0   SYSINFO [/AUTO[:*nnn*] | /DEMO] [/N] [/<u>SO</u>UND]
[/<u>SUM</u>MARY] [/TSR]

Parameters:

drive: The single-letter designator for the hard drive whose
performance you want to test in versions 4.0 and 4.5. Follow
the letter with a colon. System Information does not destroy
any information on the drive. If you do not supply a drive,
System Information does not compute a disk performance
index. In version 5.0, you cannot supply a drive letter. The
utility computes a disk performance index using the primary
hard drive (usually drive C).

/A   Skips BIOS tests. If you include this switch, System Information does not test input/output ports, check the exis-
tence of extended or expanded memory, or perform a disk
performance test.

/AUTO[:*nnn*]   Automatically cycles through all information
screens and performance tests. Use *nnn* to specify the number of seconds delay between each display or test. The default for *nnn* is 5. The cycle repeats until you press Escape to
terminate System Information. The utility ignores this switch
if you specify /DEMO, /SUMMARY, or /TSR.

/DEMO   Automatically cycles through the performance
tests, pausing approximately five seconds between each test.
The cycle repeats until you press Escape to terminate System
Information. The utility ignores this switch if you specify
/SUMMARY or /TSR.

/LOG   Displays diagnostic output as separate (not overlaid)
output lines; you can send the output to a printer or a disk
file by including the MS-DOS redirection character (>)
followed by a printer name or filename at the end of the
command.

/N   Prevents the utility from testing memory and from report-
ing information about the computer's memory. Some computers will hang and require rebooting if a memory test is
performed; however, these tests do not harm memory.

Note that early releases of version 4.0 do not process statistics about the IBM PS/2 or the VGA display mode.

/SOUND Sounds the computer's default tone between CPU speed tests.

/SUMMARY Produces a summary screen, without activating the System Information menus. If you include this switch, the utility ignores the /AUTO and /DEMO switches.

/TSR Produces a summary of terminate-and-stay-resident (TSR) programs that are active, without activating the System Information menus. If you include this switch, the utility ignores the /AUTO and /DEMO switches.

Notes:

■ When you install Norton Utilities Version 5.0, one option gives System Information a short name of SI. If you used the short name, use SI instead of SYSINFO in the syntax line above.

■ Figure 18 shows the version 5.0 initial system summary screen for System Information. Select Next to cycle through the information screens. Press F10 or use the mouse to activate any of the menus in the menu bar. The menus display information about other facets of your system or run selected tests.

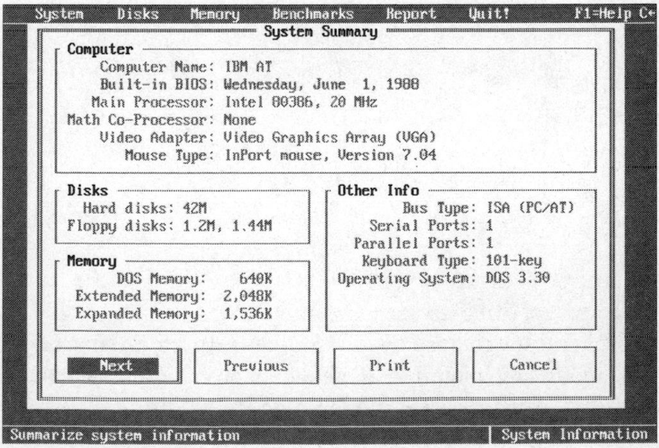

Figure 18. *System summary screen — version 5.0.*

- If you execute System Information within a multi-tasking
  environment such as Microsoft Windows, the performance benchmark results will not be accurate.

See also: DI.

TM (Time Mark)

Description:

Shows the current date and time and controls a maximum of
four independent stopwatches. You can use this command to
record and display the elapsed time for up to four independent events.

Syntax:

3.0, 3.1   TM [START] [STOP] [/C*n*] [/L] [/LOG] [/N]

4.0, 4.5   TM [START] [STOP] [*comment*] [/C*n*] [/L] [/LOG] [/N]

5.0   *See* NCC (See first item under Notes.)

Parameters:

START Resets the stopwatch and displays the time
and date.

STOP Displays the time and date and the time that has
elapsed since the last START. This keyword does not stop
the stopwatch.

comment The text string you want TM to display either
with the date and time or with the elapsed time value. TM
displays the text on the line that contains the elapsed time
value if you include the /N switch. You must enclose any
text string in quotation marks if it includes one or more
blank spaces. If the text string contains a single quotation
mark character, enclose the text in double quotation marks.
If the text string contains a double quotation mark character,
enclose the text in single quotation marks.

/Cn Selects the stopwatch that TM will use. The value for *n* can be 1 through 4. The default value is 1.

/L Displays the date and time (created with START) on the left side of the screen. If you do not include this switch, TM displays the date and time on the right side of the screen.

/LOG Displays diagnostic output as separate (not overlaid) output lines; you can send the output to a printer or a disk file by including the MS-DOS redirection character (>) followed by a printer name or filename at the end of the command.

/N Prevents TM from displaying the current time and date and shows only the elapsed time interval.

Notes:

■ If you have version 4.5 installed when you upgrade to version 5.0, the Install program does not copy TM to the 5.0 library. Copy this program yourself, especially if you have Batch Enhancer files that use this command; otherwise, you must change all uses of TM to NCC when you upgrade to version 5.0.

■ TM is incorporated into the NCC utility in version 5.0.

■ Because a stopwatch runs until you reset it with the START keyword, you can use successive STOP keywords to measure the elapsed time interval since the previous START.

■ If START follows STOP on a command line, TM displays the time that has elapsed and resets and restarts the stopwatch.

See also: NCC.

TS (Text Search)

Description:

Searches for specified text in one or more files, on an entire disk, or in the unallocated areas of a disk.

Syntax:

3.0   TS [/N]

3.1   TS [*drive*:][*path*][*filename*][*search-text*] [/EBCDIC] [/EUR]
         [/LOG] [/N] [/S] [/T]

       TS [*search-text*] {/D | /E} [/EBCDIC] [/EUR] [/LOG] [/N]

4.0   TS [*drive*:][*path*][*filename*][*search-text*] [/A] [/CS]
         [/EBCDIC] [/LOG] [/N] [/S] [/T] [/WS]

       TS [*search-text*] {/D | /E} [/A] [/CS] [/C*n*] [/EBCDIC]
         [/LOG] [/N] [/WS]

4.5   TS [*drive*:][*path*][*filename*][*search-text*] [/A] [/CS]
         [/EBCDIC] [/LOG] [/S] [/T] [/WS]

       TS [*search-text*] {/D | /E} [/A] [/CS] [/C*n*] [/EBCDIC]
         [/LOG] [/WS]

5.0   *See* FILEFIND

Parameters:

drive: The single-letter designator for the drive that contains the file you want to search. Follow the letter with a colon. The current drive is the default.

path The fully qualified name of the directory that contains the files you want to search. The current directory for the designated drive is the default.

filename The name of the file you want to search. The default *filename* is *.*.

search-text A text string for which you want to search. If the text string is more than a single word, you must enclose it in quotation marks. If the text string contains a single quotation mark character, enclose the text in double quotation marks. If the text string contains a double quotation mark character, enclose the text in single quotation marks.

/A Searches automatically by responding "yes" to all prompts.

/CS Makes the search case-sensitive. If you do not use this switch, TS ignores case when comparing *search-text* with data on disk or in a file.

/C*n* Specifies the starting cluster number when searching either the entire disk (see /D) or the erased areas on the disk (see /E).

/D Searches the entire disk, including both allocated and unallocated areas.

/E Searches the erased (unallocated) clusters in the data area.

/EBCDIC Specifies that the files you are searching use Extended Binary Coded Decimal Interchange Code rather than ASCII.

/EUR Specifies the European character set and includes character codes 128 through 255 in the search. The default is to ignore characters with a code greater than 127.

/LOG Displays diagnostic output as separate (not overlaid) output lines; you can send the output to a printer or a disk file by including the MS-DOS redirection character (>) followed by a printer name or filename at the end of the command.

/N Lets you run TS if your machine is not fully IBM-compatible. If you use this switch, you might first need to enable ANSI.SYS in the CONFIG.SYS file and then restart your computer.

/S Searches all files in all subdirectories under the current or specified path.

/T Displays the names of only the files that contain *search-text* and the total number of these files in each directory.

/WS In a WordStar input file, removes the high-order bit from all characters to restrict the search range of codes to 0 through 127. The default in versions 4.0 and 4.5 includes character codes 128 through 255 in the search.

Notes:

■ If you have version 4.5 installed prior to upgrading to version 5.0, the version 5.0 Install program allows you to copy this utility into the 5.0 subdirectory so that you can continue to use it with the new version.

■ TS is incorporated into the FILEFIND utility in version 5.0.

■ In versions 4.0 and 4.5, if you include no parameters, TS prompts you for *search-type* (file, entire disk, or erased area), for *filename* if it is performing a file search, and for *search-text*. In earlier versions, TS prompts you for *filename* and for *search-text*.

■ If you include either the /D or the /E switch, TS asks whether you want to collect clusters that contain matching data and copy the clusters to an output file. The output file must be on a drive other than the one TS is searching.

■ Use the data search feature in the NU (Norton Utility) command to scan for characters you cannot enter on the keyboard.

Example:

To search for all occurrences of "data base" in all files with the extension TXT in all directories in drive C, enter

```
TS c:\*.txt "data base" /S
```

See also: NU.

UD (Unremove Directory)

Description:

Rebuilds directories that were removed with either the
MS-DOS RMDIR command or the Norton NCD RD utility.

Syntax:

3.1   UD [*drive*:][*parent-path*]

4.0, 4.5   UD [*drive*:][*path* | *parent-path*]

5.0   *See* UNERASE

Parameters:

drive: The single-letter designator for the drive that contains
the directory you want to restore. Follow the letter with a
colon. The current drive is the default.

parent-path The name of the directory from which the lost
directory was removed. The current directory for the designated drive is the default.

path The fully qualified name of the directory that was removed. You can use the wildcard characters * and ? in the
last directory name. If you include this parameter, UD displays a screen that indicates that the specified subdirectory
has been unremoved and that identifies all files and directories in the unremoved directory that can now be unremoved
or unerased. If two or more removed directories exist that
match *path* and that are identical except for the first character, UD prompts you for a character to use for the restored
directory names so that each one is unique.

Notes:

■ UD searches for all deleted directories in *parent-path*.
   When UD finds a directory, it prompts you to confirm
   that you want to restore the directory and asks you to
   enter the missing first letter of the directory name.

■ When UD restores a directory entry, it attempts to find all
  the clusters to which the removed directory was allocated.
  If a directory was large enough to be allocated to more
  than one cluster, UD prompts you to confirm groups of
  directory entry names it finds that might have belonged to
  the directory. If UD cannot find all the directory-entry
  clusters, you might have to use NU to try to find them.

■ After UD has restored a directory, use the QU (Quick
  UnErase) command to attempt to restore the files that
  were in the directory. Use UD to attempt to restore any
  subdirectories in the newly restored directory.

■ UD is incorporated in the UNERASE command in
  version 5.0.

Example:

To restore all subdirectories that you might have removed
from the Word directory on the disk in drive A, enter

```
UD a:\word
```

See also: NU, QU.

UNERASE

Description:

Runs a full-screen menu utility that allows you to rebuild
directories that were removed with either the MS-DOS
REMOVE DIRECTORY command or the Norton NCD RD
utility. UNERASE can also recover deleted files and lost
data. UNERASE uses information in IMAGE.DAT to restore as much information about deleted files and directories
as possible (see the IMAGE command). If you also use the
FILESAVE utility, UNERASE can usually restore recently
deleted or lost files completely. If IMAGE.DAT is not available, UNERASE uses "best guess" techniques to recover
information, and lets you manually search your disk and allocate clusters to lost files or directories.

Syntax:

5.0   UNERASE [*drive*:][*path*][*filename*]

Parameters:

drive: The single-letter designator for the drive you want to use. Follow the letter with a colon. The current drive is the default.

path The fully qualified name of the directory you want to search for deleted files. The current directory for the designated drive is the default. If the path you specify does not exist, UNERASE terminates with an error. Restart UNERASE with no parameters or using the parent path of the directory you want to unerase.

filename The name of the file you want to unerase. For example, enter UNERASE *.BAT to search for all deleted files in the current directory with the extension BAT.

Notes:

■ Figure 19 on the next page shows the UNERASE screen that appears when you specify a particular path that contains erased files or directories. You can select files or directories to unerase with the spacebar or the mouse. You can choose to view allocation information about the selected file(s), view the selected file(s), or unerase them.

■ Activate the menu bar with F10 or by selecting one of the options with the mouse. The File menu provides options that let you view the current directory (the key equivalent is Alt-C), view all directories (Alt-A), change the directory (Alt-D), change the drive (Alt-R), select a file or directory (Spacebar), select a group of files or directories (gray + key on the far right of the extended keyboard), unselect a group of files or directories (gray − above the gray + key), rename a file or directory, copy the contents of an erased file to a new file on a different drive, append the contents of an erased file to another file, manually unerase a file by viewing and selecting clusters (Alt-M), or create a new file.

```
  File    Search    Options    Quit!                         F1=Help
 ╔══════════════════ Erased files in B:\TOYS ══════════════════╗
 ║                                                             ║
 ║        Name          Size      Date      Time    Prognosis  ║
 ║                                                             ║
 ║      . .             DIR    10-15-90   11:28 pm   SUB-DIR  ▲ ║
 ║      ANIMALS         DIR    10-15-90   11:29 pm   SUB-DIR    ║
 ║      BUILD           DIR    10-15-90   11:29 pm   SUB-DIR    ║
 ║      CRAFTS          DIR    10-15-90   11:29 pm   SUB-DIR    ║
 ║      GAMES           DIR    10-15-90   11:29 pm   SUB-DIR    ║
 ║      VEHICLES        DIR    10-15-90   11:29 pm   SUB-DIR    ║
 ║      ?ntro    doc    5,632   10-16-90   11:07 am   excellent  ║
 ║      ?ommand1 exe    109,568 10-17-90    4:41 pm   excellent  ║
 ║      ?ommand2 doc    63,488  10-19-90   10:02 am   excellent  ║
 ║      ?ommand3 doc    35,840  10-18-90   11:30 pm   excellent  ║
 ║      ?ppnd    doc    2,048    9-04-90   11:56 pm   excellent  ║
 ║                                                           ▼ ║
 ║                                                             ║
 ║      ┌────────┐    ┌────────┐    ┌─────────┐                ║
 ║      │  Info  │    │  View  │    │ UnErase │                ║
 ║      └────────┘    └────────┘    └─────────┘                ║
 ╚═════════════════════════════════════════════════════════════╝
 Select files to UnErase                                  UnErase
```

Figure 19.   *UNERASE display of erased files — version 5.0.*

Use the Search menu to look for specific data types (such as dBASE or Lotus), search for text, search the entire disk for a lost filename, set a range of clusters for a search, and continue a search.

From the Options menu, you can choose to sort file displays by name, extension, size, date, directory name, or recovery prognosis.

■ Because UNERASE makes a "best guess" about the clusters that originally belonged to a multiple-cluster file, the utility might not always unerase the file correctly. Use View to verify the contents of a file, and use Search and Manual Unerase (Alt-M) to correct any clusters allocated in error.

See also: FILEFIND, IMAGE, UNFORMAT.

UNFORMAT

Description:

Recovers a formatted hard disk, a disk that may have been
corrupted by a virus or a power failure, or a floppy disk that
was formatted with Norton Safe Format.

Syntax:

5.0   UNFORMAT [*drive*:]

Parameter:

drive: The single-letter designator for the drive you want to
process. Follow the letter with a colon. If you do not include
a drive letter, UNFORMAT prompts you for the drive to
process.

Notes:

■ To provide maximum protection for your system
   hard disk, include the IMAGE command in your
   AUTOEXEC.BAT file.

■ UNFORMAT cannot recover data on a floppy disk
   that was reformatted using the MS-DOS FORMAT command. Instead, reformat using the Norton Safe Format
   utility, which is available in versions 4.5 and later. Also,
   UNFORMAT cannot recover data on a floppy disk that
   was reformatted at a different density.

■ If you have not previously used the Norton IMAGE
   utility with a disk you are attempting to recover,
   UNFORMAT cannot rebuild the root directory or recover
   the files that were in the root directory. If the files on the
   disk are badly fragmented, the file allocation table (FAT)
   might be incorrect. You can avoid disk fragmentation by
   periodically executing the Speed Disk utility.

■ After you use UNFORMAT to recover a disk, you might
   need to execute the MS-DOS CHKDSK command or the

Norton NDD (Norton Disk Doctor) utility to ensure that UNFORMAT restored all files correctly. Use UNERASE to attempt further recovery on specific files.

See also: IMAGE, NDD, NU, QU, SD, SFORMAT, UD, UNERASE.

VL (Volume Label)

Description:
Displays, sets, changes, or deletes the volume label on a disk.

Syntax:
3.0   VL [*drive*:] [*label*] [/L]

3.1, 4.0, 4.5   VL [*drive*:] [*label*]

5.0   *See* NCD

Parameters:
drive: The single-letter designator for the drive you want to process. Follow the letter with a colon. The current drive is the default.

label The new label you want to place on the disk. In versions 3.1 and later, *label* can be up to 11 characters long. If *label* includes any spaces, you must enclose it within quotation marks. Version 3.0 requires a character string of up to 11 characters; any quotation marks you use become part of *label*. *label* can contain lowercase characters; if you use lowercase characters in version 3.0, include the /L switch. If you do not provide *label*, VL displays the current label and prompts you to either change or delete it.

/L Lets you include lowercase characters in *label*. If you do not include this switch in version 3.0, VL changes all lowercase characters you enter to uppercase characters.

Note:

■ VL is incorporated into the NCD utility in version 5.0.

Example:

To give the disk in drive A a label that indicates that it contains a copy of your communications software, enter

```
VL a: Commsoft
```

See also: DI, NCD, NU.

WIPEDISK

Description:

Overwrites either an entire disk or the deleted and unused areas on the disk. Overwritten data cannot be read.

Syntax:

3.0 WIPEDISK *drive*:

3.1 WIPEDISK *drive*: [/E] [/G] [/LOG] [/R*n*] [/V*n*]

4.0, 4.5 WIPEDISK *drive*: [/E] [/G*n*] [/LOG] [/R*n*] [/V*n*]

5.0 *See* WIPEINFO

Parameters:

drive: The single-letter designator for the drive you want to process. Follow the letter with a colon. You must supply the *drive*: parameter.

/E Writes over unallocated areas of the disk and does not destroy format information or current files. Unallocated areas might contain data from files that have been deleted; use this switch to ensure that deleted files cannot be read again.

/G Follows U.S. government erasing standards for writing over data. If you include this switch, WIPEDISK writes binary 1s (hexadecimal FF) on the first pass, binary 0s on the

second pass, and either a default value of 246 (hexadecimal
F6) or the value you specify with the /V switch on the third
pass. After the third write pass, WIPEDISK read-verifies the
last value written. In versions 4.0 and 4.5, you can specify
the number of times you want WIPEDISK to repeat the first
two write passes by adding a number to the /G switch; the
default number for *n* is 3. In versions 3.1, 4.0, and 4.5, you
can use the /R switch to specify the number of times you
want WIPEDISK to repeat the entire write-over cycle.

/LOG Displays diagnostic output as separate (not overlaid)
output; you can send the output to a printer or a disk file by
including the MS-DOS redirection character (>) followed by
a printer name or filename at the end of the command.

/R*n* Repeats the write passes *n* times. The default value is 1.

/V*n* Uses the binary equivalent of the decimal value *n* when
writing over data. If you do not use the /G switch, the default
value is 0.

Notes:

■ The MS-DOS DELETE and ERASE commands do not
destroy data or completely remove directory entries. To
ensure that data is completely erased and cannot be reused, you must use WIPEDISK or WIPEFILE.

■ When you use WIPEDISK to write over an entire disk,
the command writes over all data, including the format information (unless you use the /E switch). You must reformat the disk before you can use it again.

Caution: *When you use WIPEDISK to write over data,
you cannot recover the data by using the FR (Format
Recover), the NU (Norton Utilities), or the QU (Quick
UnErase) command. WIPEDISK always asks for confirmation before it begins execution. If you discover you
have started WIPEDISK by mistake, you can halt
execution by pressing Ctrl-C or Ctrl-Break. WIPEDISK
begins erasing from the last track on the disk, so halting
the execution of WIPEDISK quickly might save much of
your data.*

- WIPEDISK is incorporated in the WIPEINFO command in version 5.0.

Example:

To use U.S. government erasing standards to write over the data that might have been stored in currently unallocated areas on the disk in drive B, enter

```
WIPEDISK b: /E /G
```

See also: FR, NU, QU, UD, WIPEFILE, WIPEINFO.

WIPEFILE

Description:

Overwrites selected files, the space allocated to the files, and the files' directory entries. You can also use this command to delete files.

Syntax:

3.0   WIPEFILE [*drive*:][*path*][*filename*] [/D] [/N] [/P]

3.1   WIPEFILE [*drive*:][*path*][*filename*] [/G] [/LOG] [/N] [/NOD] [/P] [/R*n*] [/V*n*]

4.0, 4.5   WIPEFILE [*drive*:][*path*]*filename* [/G*n*] [/LOG] [/N] [/P] [/R*n*] [/S] [/V*n*]

5.0   *See* WIPEINFO

Parameters:

drive: The single-letter designator for the drive you want to use. Follow the letter with a colon. If you do not specify *drive* and you specify either *path*, *filename*, or both, the current drive is the default.

path The fully qualified name of the directory that contains the files you want to write over and/or delete. The current directory on the selected drive is the default.

filename The name of the file you want to write over and/or
delete. If you provide *drive*: or *path* in versions 3.0 and 3.1,
the default *filename* is *.*. You must supply *filename* in versions 4.0 and 4.5.

/D Deletes the file after it has been overwritten.

/G Follows U.S. government erasing standards for writing
over data. If you include this switch, WIPEFILE writes binary 1s (hexadecimal FF) on the first pass, binary 0s on the
second pass, and either a default value of 246 (hexadecimal
F6) or the value you specify with the /V switch on the third
pass. After the third write pass, WIPEFILE read-verifies the
last value written. In versions 4.0 and 4.5, you can specify
the number of times you want WIPEFILE to repeat the first
two write passes by adding a number to the /G switch; the
default number for *n* is 3. In versions 3.1, 4.0, and 4.5, you
can use the /R switch to specify the number of times you
want WIPEFILE to repeat the entire write-over cycle.

/LOG Displays diagnostic output as separate (not overlaid)
output; you can send the output to a printer or a disk file by
including the MS-DOS redirection character (>) followed by
a printer name or filename at the end of the command.

/N Deletes (erases) files but does not write over their allocated areas or their directory entries. If you supply this
switch, WIPEFILE removes files the same way the MS-DOS
command DELETE or ERASE does.

/NOD Writes over the allocated file clusters but does not
free the space allocated to the files or erase the directory
entries.

/P Pauses for confirmation before writing over or deleting
each file.

/R*n* Repeats the write passes *n* times. The default value is 1.

/S Writes over all files in all directories under the specified
path.

/V*n* Uses the binary equivalent of the decimal value *n* when
writing over data. If you do not include the /G switch, the
default value is 0.

Notes:

■ The MS-DOS DELETE and ERASE commands do not
destroy data or completely remove directory entries. To
ensure that data is completely erased and cannot be reused, you must use WIPEDISK or WIPEFILE.

Caution: *When you use WIPEFILE to write over data,
you cannot recover the data using the FR (Format
Recover), the NU (Norton Utilities), or the QU (Quick
UnErase) command. WIPEFILE always asks for confirmation before it begins execution. If you discover you
have started WIPEFILE by mistake, you can halt execution by pressing Ctrl-C or Ctrl-Break.*

■ WIPEFILE processes hidden and system files. If *filename*
might include any such files, be sure to include the /P
switch so that you can prevent WIPEFILE from deleting
and/or writing over them.

■ WIPEFILE bypasses read-only files unless you instruct it
to remove the read-only attribute before processing the
file. WIPEFILE prompts you to confirm that you want to
remove the read-only attribute only if you instruct the utility to pause before processing each file. You can do so in
any version by including the /P switch, by responding
"Y" to the initial message that asks "Do you wish confirmation for each file (Y/N)?" in versions 4.0 and 4.5, or by
responding "N" to the initial message that asks "Proceed
without pausing (Y/N)?" in versions 3.0 and 3.1.

■ WIPEFILE is incorporated in the WIPEINFO command
in version 5.0.

Example:

To delete all files with the extension LOG in the GAMES
directory and to write over the data and directory entries,
pausing for confirmation before processing each file, enter

```
WIPEFILE \games\*.log /P
```

See also: FA, FR, NU, QU, UD, WIPEDISK, WIPEINFO.

WIPEINFO

Description:

Overwrites selected files, the space allocated to files, the slack space at the end of files, files' directory entries, an entire disk, or the deleted and unused areas on a disk. Overwritten data cannot be read or recovered. You can also use this utility to delete files without overwriting them.

Syntax:

5.0   WIPEINFO [*drive*:] [/E] [/G*n*] [/R*n*] [/V*n*]

WIPEINFO [*drive*:][*path*][*filename*] [/G*n*] [/K] [/N] [/R*n*] [/S] [/V*n*]

Parameters:

drive: The single-letter designator for the drive you want to process. Follow the letter with a colon. The default is the current drive. If you provide only a drive letter and no *path* or *filename*, WIPEINFO assumes you want to erase the entire disk, but prompts you for confirmation before proceeding.

path The fully qualified name of the directory that contains the files you want to write over and/or delete. The current directory on the selected drive is the default.

filename The name of the file you want to write over and/or delete. If you provide a *drive*: or *path*, the default *filename* is *.*. WIPEINFO prompts you to confirm your selection before proceeding.

/E When you specify only a *drive*:, writes over unallocated areas of the disk and does not destroy format information or current files. Unallocated areas might contain data from files that have been deleted. Use this switch to ensure that deleted files cannot be read again.

/G*n* Follows U.S. government erasing standards for writing over data. If you include this switch, WIPEINFO writes binary 1s (hexadecimal FF) on the first pass, binary 0s on the second pass, and either a default value of 246 (hexadecimal F6) or the value you specify with the /V switch on the third pass. After the third write pass, WIPEINFO read-verifies the last value written. You can specify the number of times you want WIPEINFO to repeat the first two write passes by adding a number to the /G switch; the default number for *n* is 3. You can also use the /R switch to specify the number of times you want WIPEINFO to repeat the entire write-over cycle.

/K Writes over the slack space at the end of the specified file(s). Since space on a disk is allocated in fixed clusters, the last cluster in a file is not usually full. WIPEINFO makes sure that any leftover data in the "empty" part of the last cluster of a file cannot be read. This space might contain usable data from deleted files.

/N Deletes (erases) files but does not write over their allocated areas or their directory entries. If you supply this switch, WIPEINFO removes files the same way the MS-DOS command DELETE or ERASE does.

/R*n* Repeats the write passes *n* times. The default value is 1.

/S Writes over all files in all directories under the specified path.

/V*n* Uses the binary equivalent of the decimal value *n* when writing over data. If you do not include the /G switch, the default value is 0. When you include the /G switch, providing a different /V value may not meet government standards.

Notes:

■ The MS-DOS DELETE and ERASE commands do not destroy data or completely remove directory entries. To ensure that data is completely erased and cannot be reused, you must use WIPEINFO.

Caution: *When you use WIPEINFO to write over data, you cannot recover the data using the UNERASE or UNFORMAT command. WIPEINFO always asks for confirmation before it begins execution. If you discover you have started WIPEINFO by mistake, you can halt execution by pressing Escape, Ctrl-C, or Ctrl-Break. When erasing an entire disk, WIPEINFO begins erasing from the last track on the disk, so halting the execution of WIPEINFO quickly might save much of your data.*

■ When you use WIPEINFO to write over an entire disk, the command writes over all data, including the format information (unless you use the /E switch). You must reformat the disk before you can use it again.

■ When you use WIPEINFO to write over a drive, the Wipe Drives dialog box appears. Use the dialog box as needed to select or change the drive or the writing method (entire drive or unused areas only). Select Wipe to begin writing over the drive.

■ When you use WIPEINFO to write over files, the Wipe Files dialog box appears. Use the dialog box to specify or change the filename and to include or exclude subdirectories, hidden files, and read-only files. Check the Confirm each file box if you are writing over several files, particularly when you specify files with wildcard characters, to prevent accidental writing over of files you need to keep. You can also specify or change the writing method (wipe files, Delete files only, don't wipe, or wipe unused file slack only). Use Directory to list other directories, and use Wipe to begin writing over files.

■ WIPEINFO processes system files. If *filename* might include any such files, be sure to select "Confirm each file" in the Wipe Files dialog box so that you can prevent WIPEINFO from deleting and/or writing over them.

■ You can establish WIPEINFO defaults by starting WIPEINFO with no parameters, selecting Options from the Wipe Drives, Wipe Files, and Wipe Configuration dialog boxes, and selecting Save settings from the Wipe Configuration dialog box.

■ WIPEINFO bypasses read-only and hidden files unless you instruct it to write over these files in the Wipe Files dialog box. In early copies of version 5.0, WIPEINFO erroneously removes the read-only attribute regardless of your selection.

Example:

To delete all files with the extension LOG in the GAMES directory and to write over the data and directory entries, enter

```
WIPEINFO \games\*.log
```

See also: FA, FILEFIND, FR, NU, QU, UD, UNERASE, UNFORMAT, WIPEFILE, WIPEDISK.

Appendixes

Appendix A

Recovery Scenarios

The following table lists several common problems and the utilities you can use to correct them. The utilities are listed in the order in which you should use them.

Problem	Utility to use
File deleted	QU (with versions 3.1, 4.0, and 4.5), UNERASE (with version 5.0); if unsuccessful, NU (versions 4.5 and earlier)
Directory removed	UD (with versions 3.1, 4.0, and 4.5), UNERASE (with version 5.0); then recover deleted files
Disk formatted erroneously	FR (with versions 4.0 and 4.5, Advanced Edition only), UNFORMAT (with version 5.0); NDD
Data in bad cluster	DT with /M switch (with versions 4.0 and 4.5), NDD and DISKTOOL (version 5.0)
DOS Recover run erroneously	FR, NU (with versions 4.0 and 4.5, Advanced Edition—these utilities work best if you have previously run FR /SAVE or DP on the disk); DISKTOOL, UNERASE, NDD (with version 5.0—these utilities work best if you have previously run IMAGE on the disk)

(continued)

(continued)

Problem	Utility to use
Format run erroneously	FR, NU (with versions 4.0 and 4.5, Advanced Edition—these utilities work best if you have previously run FR /SAVE or DP on the disk); UNFORMAT, UNERASE, NDD (with version 5.0—these utilities work best if you have previously run IMAGE on the disk)
File hidden	FA (with versions 3.1, 4.0, and 4.5); FILEFIND (with version 5.0)
Read-only file marked or unmarked	FA (with versions 4.5 and earlier); FILEFIND (with version 5.0)

Appendix B

A Sample Menu System Using Version 5.0 Batch Enhancer

The following examples show you how to use the Batch Enhancer in version 5.0 of the Norton Utilities to create a menu selection system for the tasks you perform most often. The menu system requires MS-DOS version 3.3 or later. Several commands expect these batch files to reside in a \MENUSYS directory. Modify all references to \MENUSYS if you want to create the examples in a different directory. The batch files whose filenames appear in lowercase are not provided—you must create appropriate batch files on your system to start your database, word processor, and so on.

MENU.BAT   The main program

```
@ ECHO OFF
:AGAIN
REM  Establish root directory
CD \
REM  Clear the screen
CLS
REM  Have BE display the main menu
BE \MENUSYS\MENU1.DAT

REM  Ask for one-character
REM  response — default is Quit
BE ASK " " QWSMGDC DEF=Q BRIGHT YELLOW

REM  Check response and go do what was asked
IF ERRORLEVEL 7 GOTO COMM
IF ERRORLEVEL 6 GOTO DBASE
IF ERRORLEVEL 5 GOTO GAMES
IF ERRORLEVEL 4 GOTO MONEY
IF ERRORLEVEL 3 GOTO SPREAD
IF ERRORLEVEL 2 GOTO WORD
IF ERRORLEVEL 1 GOTO QUIT
```

```
:COMM
REM  Call the communications options batch file
CALL \MENUSYS\COMM.BAT
REM  After exit, return and repaint the main menu
GOTO AGAIN

:DBASE
REM  Call your database start-up batch file
CALL db.bat
REM  After exit, return and repaint the main menu
GOTO AGAIN

:GAMES
REM  Call the games options batch file
CALL \MENUSYS\GAMES.BAT
REM  After exit, return and repaint the main menu
GOTO AGAIN

:MONEY
REM  Call your money manager batch file
CALL money.bat
REM  After exit, return and repaint the main menu
GOTO AGAIN

:SPREAD
REM  Call your spreadsheet start-up batch file
CALL spread.bat
REM  After exit, return and repaint the main menu
GOTO AGAIN

:WORD
REM  Call the word-processing options batch file
CALL \MENUSYS\WORDSUB.BAT
REM  After exit, return and repaint the main menu
GOTO AGAIN

:QUIT
REM  Repaint the screen, then end

REM  Paint a red border (CGA or VGA only)
BE SA ON RED
REM  Then set up white text on blue background
BE SA BRIGHT WHITE ON BLUE /C /N
EXIT
```

MENU1.DAT   The main menu

```
REM   Reset base screen attributes
SA NORMAL
SA ON BLUE

REM   Zoom up the main menu
WINDOW 2,4,22,75 BRIGHT YELLOW ON MAGENTA ZOOM
REM   Overlay yellow border with blue (writing in
REM   window still yellow)
BOX 2,4,22,75 SINGLE BRIGHT BLUE

REM   Write in the text and choices
ROWCOL 5,30 "CUSTOM PC MENU SYSTEM"
ROWCOL 7,25 "Options:" BRIGHT YELLOW
REM   Note option letters are highlighted
REM   in different color
ROWCOL 9,25 "C" BRIGHT YELLOW
ROWCOL 9,26 "ommunications programs" BRIGHT WHITE
ROWCOL 10,25 "D" BRIGHT YELLOW
ROWCOL 10,26 "ata base management" BRIGHT WHITE
ROWCOL 11,25 "G" BRIGHT YELLOW
ROWCOL 11 26 "ames to play" BRIGHT WHITE
ROWCOL 12,25 "M" BRIGHT YELLOW
ROWCOL 12,26 "oney management" BRIGHT WHITE
ROWCOL 13,25 "S" BRIGHT YELLOW
ROWCOL 13,26 "preadsheet" BRIGHT WHITE
ROWCOL 14,25 "W" BRIGHT YELLOW
ROWCOL 14,26 "ord processor" BRIGHT WHITE
ROWCOL 15,25 "Q" BRIGHT YELLOW
ROWCOL 15,26 "uit — exit to DOS" BRIGHT WHITE

REM   Prompt for user input
ROWCOL 18,20 "Press option letter..." BRIGHT YELLOW
```

COMM.BAT   Called by MENU.BAT

```
REM   Communications subroutine:

REM   Paint the communications submenu
BE \MENUSYS\MENUC.DAT
REM   Ask for one-character
REM   response — default is Quit
BE ASK " " BEMSQ DEF=Q BRIGHT GREEN
```

```
REM   Check response and go do what was asked
IF ERRORLEVEL 5 GOTO DONE
IF ERRORLEVEL 4 GOTO SHOP
IF ERRORLEVEL 3 GOTO QUOTES
IF ERRORLEVEL 2 GOTO EMAIL

:BULLET
REM   Start a timer
NCC /START:1 /N
REM   Call your bulletin board connect routine
CALL bullet.bat
REM   Go Log elapsed time and exit
GOTO CEXIT

:EMAIL
REM   Start a timer
NCC /START:1 /N
REM   Call your electronic mail connect routine
CALL email.bat
REM   Go Log elapsed time and exit
GOTO CEXIT

:QUOTES
REM   Start a timer
NCC /START:1 /N
REM   Call your stock quotes connect routine
CALL stock.bat
REM   Go Log elapsed time and exit
GOTO CEXIT

:SHOP
REM   Start a timer
NCC /START:1 /N
REM   Call your on-line shopping connect routine
CALL shop.bat
REM   Go Log elapsed time and exit
GOTO CEXIT

:CEXIT
REM   Restore the menus
BE \MENUSYS\MENU1.DAT
BE \MENUSYS\MENUC.DAT
BE ROWCOL 17,22 "Exit from Communications"
```

```
BE ROWCOL 18,22
REM  And show elapsed time
NCC /C:"Connect elapsed time: "/STOP:1 /N /L
BE ROWCOL 19,22
BE ASK "Press any key to continue..." TIMEOUT=15

:DONE
```

MENUC.DAT   Menu invoked by COMM.BAT

```
REM  Overlay the communications options window
WINDOW 6,15,19,65 BRIGHT GREEN ON RED ZOOM SHADOW
REM  Write in the menu options
ROWCOL 9,22 "Choose a service:" BRIGHT GREEN
REM  Note option letters are highlighted
REM  in different color
ROWCOL 11,25 "B" BRIGHT GREEN
ROWCOL 11,26 "ulletin Board" BRIGHT WHITE
ROWCOL 12,25 "E" BRIGHT GREEN
ROWCOL 12,26 "lectronic Mail" BRIGHT WHITE
ROWCOL 13,25 "M" BRIGHT GREEN
ROWCOL 13,26 "arket Quotes (stocks)" BRIGHT WHITE
ROWCOL 14,25 "S" BRIGHT GREEN
ROWCOL 14,26 "hopping online" BRIGHT WHITE
ROWCOL 15,25 "Q" BRIGHT GREEN
ROWCOL 15,26 "uit — exit to main menu" BRIGHT WHITE

REM  Prompt for user input
ROWCOL 17,22 "Press option letter ..." BRIGHT GREEN
```

GAMES.BAT   Called by MENU.BAT

```
REM  Games subroutine:

:START
REM  Paint the primary games submenu
BE \MENUSYS\MENUG.DAT
REM  Ask for one-character
REM  response — default is Quit
BE ASK " " ABDQ DEF=Q BRIGHT RED

REM  Check response and go do what was asked
IF ERRORLEVEL 4 GOTO DONE
IF ERRORLEVEL 3 GOTO QUESTS
IF ERRORLEVEL 2 GOTO BOARD
```

```
:ARCADE
REM  Call the arcade games options batch file
CALL \MENUSYS\ARCADE.BAT
REM  After return, repaint the main menu
BE \MENUSYS\MENU1.DAT
REM  Display the primary games submenu
GOTO START

:BOARD
REM  Call the board games options batch file
CALL \MENUSYS\BOARD.BAT
REM  After return, repaint the main menu
BE \MENUSYS\MENU1.DAT
REM  Display the primary games submenu
GOTO START

:QUESTS
REM  Call the adventure games options batch file
CALL \MENUSYS\QUESTS.BAT
REM  After return, repaint the main menu
BE \MENUSYS\MENU1.DAT
REM  Display the primary games submenu
GOTO START

:DONE
```

MENUG.DAT   Menu invoked by GAMES.BAT

```
REM  Overlay the main games options window
WINDOW 6,10,17,51 RED ON GREEN ZOOM SHADOW

REM  Write in the menu options
ROWCOL 8,15 "Choose a game category:" RED
REM  Note option letters are highlighted in
REM  different color
ROWCOL 10,17 "A" RED
ROWCOL 10,18 "rcade games" BRIGHT WHITE
ROWCOL 11,17 "B" RED
ROWCOL 11,18 "oard games" BRIGHT WHITE
ROWCOL 12,17 "Adventure games" BRIGHT WHITE
ROWCOL 12,18 "d" RED
ROWCOL 13,17 "Q" RED
ROWCOL 13,18 "uit — exit to main menu" BRIGHT WHITE

REM  Prompt for user input
ROWCOL 15,12 "Press option letter ..." RED
```

ARCADE.BAT   Called by GAMES.BAT

```
REM   Arcade games subroutine:

:START
REM   Paint the arcade games submenu
BE \MENUSYS\MENUGA.DAT
REM   Ask for one-character
REM   response — default is Quit
BE ASK " " FJPQ DEF=Q BRIGHT CYAN

REM   Check response and go do what was asked
IF ERRORLEVEL 4 GOTO DONE
IF ERRORLEVEL 3 GOTO FROG
IF ERRORLEVEL 2 GOTO JETS

:PONG
REM   Call your pong game
CALL pong.bat
REM   After return, repaint the main menu
BE \MENUSYS\MENU1.DAT
REM   Then restore the games menu
GOTO DONE

:JETS
REM   Call your flying game
CALL jets.bat
REM   After return, repaint the main menu
BE \MENUSYS\MENU1.DAT
REM   Then restore the games menu
GOTO DONE

:FROG
REM   Call your frog game
CALL frog.bat
REM   After return, repaint the main menu
BE \MENUSYS\MENU1.DAT
REM   Then restore the games menu

:DONE
```

MENUGA.DAT   Menu invoked by ARCADE.BAT

```
REM  Overlay the arcade games suboptions window
WINDOW 8,20,19,61 BRIGHT CYAN ON RED ZOOM SHADOW

REM  Write in the menu options
ROWCOL 10,25 "Choose an Arcade game:" BRIGHT CYAN
REM  Note option letters are highlighted in
REM  different color
ROWCOL 12,27 "F" BRIGHT CYAN
ROWCOL 12,28 "rog jump" BRIGHT WHITE
ROWCOL 13,27 "J" BRIGHT CYAN
ROWCOL 13,28 "et fighter pilot" BRIGHT WHITE
ROWCOL 14,27 "P" BRIGHT CYAN
ROWCOL 14,28 "ing-Pong" BRIGHT WHITE
ROWCOL 15,27 "Q" BRIGHT CYAN
ROWCOL 15,28 "uit — exit to games menu" BRIGHT WHITE

REM  Prompt for user input
ROWCOL 17,22 "Press option letter ..." BRIGHT CYAN
```

BOARD.BAT   Called by GAMES.BAT

```
REM  Board games subroutine:

:START
REM  Paint the board games submenu
BE \MENUSYS\MENUGB.DAT
REM  Ask for one-character
REM  response — default is Quit
BE ASK " " BCGQ DEF=Q BRIGHT CYAN

REM  Check response and go do what was asked
IF ERRORLEVEL 4 GOTO DONE
IF ERRORLEVEL 3 GOTO GO
IF ERRORLEVEL 2 GOTO CHECK

:BACKG
REM  Call your backgammon game
CALL backg.bat
REM  After exit, return and repaint the main menu
BE \MENUSYS\MENU1.DAT
REM  Then restore the games menu
GOTO DONE
```

```
:CHECK
REM  Call your checkers game
CALL checker.bat
REM  After return, repaint the main menu
BE \MENUSYS\MENU1.DAT
REM  Then restore the games menu
GOTO DONE

:GO
REM  Call your "GO" game
CALL go.bat
REM  After return, repaint the main menu
BE \MENUSYS\MENU1.DAT
REM  Then restore the games menu

:DONE
```

MENUGB.DAT   Menu invoked by BOARD.BAT

```
REM  Overlay the board games suboptions window
WINDOW 8,20,19,61 BRIGHT CYAN ON RED ZOOM SHADOW

REM  Write in the menu options
ROWCOL 10,25 "Choose a board game:" BRIGHT CYAN
REM  Note option letters are highlighted
REM  in different color
ROWCOL 12,27 "B" BRIGHT CYAN
ROWCOL 12,28 "ackgammon" BRIGHT WHITE
ROWCOL 13,27 "C" BRIGHT CYAN
ROWCOL 13,28 "heckers" BRIGHT WHITE
ROWCOL 14,27 "G" BRIGHT CYAN
ROWCOL 14,28 "o" BRIGHT WHITE
ROWCOL 15,27 "Q" BRIGHT CYAN
ROWCOL 15,28 "uit — exit to games menu" BRIGHT WHITE

REM  Prompt for user input
ROWCOL 17,22 "Press option letter ..." BRIGHT CYAN
```

QUESTS.BAT   Called by GAMES.BAT

```
REM  Adventure games subroutine:

:START
REM  Paint the adventure games submenu
BE \MENUSYS\MENUGQ.DAT
REM  Ask for one-character
REM  response — default is Quit
BE ASK " " 123Q DEF=Q BRIGHT CYAN
```

```
REM  Check response and go do what was asked
IF ERRORLEVEL 4 GOTO DONE
IF ERRORLEVEL 3 GOTO THREE
IF ERRORLEVEL 2 GOTO TWO

:ONE
REM  Call your Quest1 game
CALL quest1.bat
REM  After return, repaint the main menu
BE \MENUSYS\MENU1.DAT
REM  Then restore the games menu
GOTO DONE

:TWO
REM  Call your Quest2 game
CALL quest2.bat
REM  After return, repaint the main menu
BE \MENUSYS\MENU1.DAT
REM  Then restore the games menu
GOTO DONE

:THREE
REM  Call your Quest3 game
CALL quest3.bat
REM  After return, repaint the main menu
BE \MENUSYS\MENU1.DAT
REM  Then restore the games menu

:DONE
```

MENUGQ.DAT   Menu invoked by QUESTS.BAT

```
REM  Overlay the adventure games suboptions window
WINDOW 8,20,19,61 BRIGHT CYAN ON RED ZOOM SHADOW

REM  Write in the menu options...
ROWCOL 10,25 "Choose a game:" BRIGHT CYAN
REM  Note option letters are highlighted in
REM  different color
ROWCOL 12,27 "Quest 1 - Goblins" BRIGHT WHITE
ROWCOL 12,33 "1" BRIGHT CYAN
ROWCOL 13,27 "Quest 2 - Dragons" BRIGHT WHITE
ROWCOL 13,33 "2" BRIGHT CYAN
ROWCOL 14,27 "Quest 3 - Minotaurs" BRIGHT WHITE
ROWCOL 14,33 "3" BRIGHT CYAN
ROWCOL 15,27 "Q" BRIGHT CYAN
ROWCOL 15,28 "uit - exit to games menu" BRIGHT WHITE
```

```
REM  Prompt for user input...
ROWCOL 17,22 "Press option letter ..." BRIGHT CYAN
```

WORDSUB.BAT   Called by MENU.BAT

```
REM  Word-processing subroutine

REM  Paint the word options menu
BE \MENUSYS\MENUW.DAT
REM  Ask for one-character
REM  response — default is Quit
BE ASK " " MDJSQ DEF=Q BRIGHT RED

IF ERRORLEVEL 5 GOTO DONE
IF ERRORLEVEL 4 GOTO SIS
IF ERRORLEVEL 3 GOTO JUNIOR
IF ERRORLEVEL 2 GOTO DAD

:MOM
REM  Call word processor with mom's subdirectory
CD \WORD\MOM
CALL word.bat
CD \
GOTO DONE

:DAD
REM  Call word processor with dad's subdirectory
CD \WORD\DAD
CALL word.bat
CD \
GOTO DONE

:JUNIOR
REM  Call word processor with junior's subdirectory
CD \WORD\JUNIOR
CALL word.bat
CD \
GOTO DONE

:SIS
REM  Call word processor with sis's subdirectory
CD \WORD\SIS
CALL word.bat
CD \

:DONE
```

MENUW.DAT   Menu invoked by WORDSUB.BAT

```
REM   Overlay the word processor's
REM   subdirectory options menu
WINDOW 6,15,19,65 BRIGHT RED ON BLUE ZOOM SHADOW
REM   Write in the menu options
ROWCOL 9,28 "Choose a text sublibrary:" BRIGHT RED
REM   Note option letters are highlighted in
REM   different color
ROWCOL 11,23 "M" BRIGHT RED
ROWCOL 11,24 "om's library" BRIGHT WHITE
ROWCOL 12,23 "D" BRIGHT RED
ROWCOL 12,24 "ad's library" BRIGHT WHITE
ROWCOL 13,23 "J" BRIGHT RED
ROWCOL 13,24 "unior's library" BRIGHT WHITE
ROWCOL 14,23 "S" BRIGHT RED
ROWCOL 14,24 "is's library" BRIGHT WHITE
ROWCOL 15,23 "Q" BRIGHT RED
ROWCOL 15,24 "uit — return to main menu" BRIGHT WHITE

REM   Prompt for user input
ROWCOL 17,23 "Press option letter ..." BRIGHT RED
```

Appendix C

BEEP Note Frequencies

Frequency	Note	Frequency	Note
131	C	554	C#
138	C#	587	D
147	D	622	D#
155	D#	659	E
165	E	698	F
175	F	740	F#
185	F#	784	G
196	G	831	G#
208	G#	880	A
220	A	932	A#
233	A#	988	B
247	B	1047	C
262	C (Middle C)	1109	C#
277	C#	1175	D
294	D	1245	D#
311	D#	1319	E
330	E	1397	F
349	F	1480	F#
370	F#	1568	G
392	G	1661	G#
415	G#	1760	A
440	A	1865	A#
466	A#	1976	B
494	B	2093	C
523	C		

Appendix D

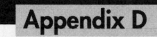 Color Names and Codes

Color names for BE SA and SA commands:

WHITE	BLACK	RED	MAGENTA
BLUE	GREEN	CYAN	YELLOW

Note that all color names may be abbreviated to their first three or more letters.

Color codes for /F*n* and /B*n* switches:

n	Color
0	black
1	blue
2	green
3	cyan
4	red
5	magenta
6	brown
7	white
8	gray (light black)
9	light blue
10	light green
11	light cyan
12	pink (light red)
13	light magenta
14	yellow (light brown)
15	bright white

JOHN L. VIESCAS

John L. Viescas, a specialist in systems analysis and relational database management systems, is a consultant for Tandem Computers, Incorporated. He has more than 23 years of industry experience, including information security management and mainframe database software product development. He regularly conducts seminars on relational databases and SQL relational database language for Tandem customers, Tandem third-party vendors, and industry consultants who specialize in PC-mainframe cooperative processing issues. He has been a guest lecturer for the Association for Computing Machinery (ACM), the Data Administration Management Association (DAMA), and college-level classes in data processing concepts. Viescas graduated *cum laude* from the University of Texas at Dallas with a degree in business finance. He resides in Redmond, Washington, with his wife and one of their seven children.

The manuscript for this book was prepared and submitted to Microsoft Press in electronic form. Text files were processed and formatted using Microsoft Word.

Principal word processor: Sean Donahue
Principal proofreader: Camilla Ayers
Principal typographer: Michelle Neil
Interior text designer: Darcie S. Furlan
Cover designer: Celeste Design
Cover color separator: Rainier Color Corporation

Text composition by Editorial Services of New England, Inc. in Times Roman with display in Futura Heavy, using Xerox Ventura Publisher and the Compugraphic 9600.